A China Diary

中华人民共和国外交部

以色列国驻华大使馆

The 'envelope' conveying the first official communication from China's Foreign Ministry to the new Israeli Embassy in Beijing

A China Diary

Towards the establishment of China–Israel diplomatic relations

E. ZEV SUFOTT

FRANK CASS
LONDON • PORTLAND, OR

First Published in 1997 in Great Britain by
FRANK CASS & CO. LTD.
Newbury House, 900 Eastern Avenue
London IG2 7HH

and in the United States of America by
FRANK CASS
c/o ISBS, 5804 N.E. Hassalo Street
Portland, Oregon 97213-3644

British Library Cataloguing in Publication Data:

Sufott, E. Zev
 A China diary : Towards the establishment of China–Israel
diplomatic relations
 1. Israel – Foreign relations – China 2. China – Foreign
relations – Israel – 1949–
 I. Title
 327.5'694'051

ISBN 0 7146 4721 7 (cloth)
ISBN 0 7146 4271 1 (paper)

Library of Congress Cataloging-in-Publication Data:

Sufott, E. Zev, 1927–
 A China diary : Towards the establishment of China–Israel
diplomatic relations
  p. cm.
 Includes bibliographical references.
 ISBN 0-7146-4721-7 (cloth). — ISBN 0-7146-4271-1 (pbk)
 1. Israel—Foreign relations—China. 2. China—Foreign relations—
Israel. 3. Sufott, E. Zev, 1927–   . 4. Diplomats—Israel—
Biography. I. Title.
DS119.8.C5S84 1997
327.5105694—dc21   96-52662

Typeset by
Vitaset, Paddock Wood

Printed in Great Britain by
Bookcraft (Bath) Ltd, Midsomer Norton, Avon

Contents

List of Illustrations

Prologue

THE FIRST official exchange between the People's Republic of China and the State of Israel was in January 1950, some months after the establishment of the Communist regime in Beijing. On 9 January 1950, Israel's Foreign Minister, Moshe Sharett, informed his Chinese counterpart, Zhou Enlai, in the customary cabled message, of Israel's recognition of China's new government as the legitimate regime. This is the step required of a pre-existing state, conferring recognition upon a new state or regime. A week later, on 16 January 1950, the customary cable of acknowledgement was received in Jerusalem. Over 40 years were to elapse before the normalization of relations between the two countries. In the intervening decades, contacts between China and Israel were few and far between. The only occurrence of continuous contacts was between Israel's first Minister to Burma and his Chinese counterpart, starting early in 1954 and culminating in the visit of an official Israeli delegation to China early in 1955. These could well have led to normalization and the establishment of diplomatic relations, as the records suggest.[1] Post-Korean War China was seeking to extend the range of its relations and define an international role for itself.

Washington DC was exerting its influence against relations and contacts with China. It remains a moot point to what extent this inhibited Jerusalem. The Israeli government's instructions to its Minister in Rangoon and to the Israeli delegation which visited China contained explicit cautions against any commitments beyond the exploration of possibilities for bilateral trade. Development of

---

1. David Hacohen, *Burma Diary 1953–1955* (Tel Aviv: Am Oved, 1963), pp.417–18.

these contacts was cut short by the Bandung Conference of non-aligned states, held in Indonesia in April 1955, which marked an evolution in the international role which China was to set for itself, and in its perception of its relations with the Arab and Moslem states. China was made fully aware, even in the early stages leading up to the Conference, of the Arab states' demand for the boycott of all relations with Israel.

Over the following three decades, China could be placed in a category of its own, as far as Israel was concerned. Only very rare cases are recorded of Chinese entry visas issued to bearers of Israeli passports. The rule was that Israeli passport holders were not granted entry to China. Official communication between the two countries was even rarer. A unique Chinese Diplomatic Note was addressed to Israel in August 1963, on the subject of nuclear disarmament. Israel had possibly been included by error in the list of recipients of the Chinese Note. Israel's detailed response, including proposals for exchanges and relations between the two countries, was met with a deafening silence. This did not deter the Israeli government from despatching a follow-up Note of reminder, which likewise elicited no acknowledgement.

Direct trade with Israel was forbidden, unlike trade relations between China and other countries with which China had no official relations but conducted lively trade exchanges, including some of Israel's Arab neighbours. Postal contacts were, at best, haphazard. The very suggestion, in a press report in the early 1970s, that telephone links were to be established between the two countries, elicited a firm Chinese denial of any such links with the 'Zionist entity', this being the official Chinese designation for the State of Israel during that period.

In fact, there was no official contact between the two governments for over 30 years, from the time of the Israeli delegation's visit to China in February 1955 until the first meeting between the two countries' Foreign Ministers, at the UN General Assembly session in September 1987. As far as China was concerned, it acceded, in the framework of its obligations as a Permanent Member of the Security Council, to Israel's 1987 request for a meeting between the two Ministers, and in their roles as Heads of Delegations to the UN General Assembly, rather than to bilateral contacts between the two states or governments. This first meeting of its kind had been preceded by several diplomatic contacts at a lower level, as reported in the press. It followed press reports of secret exchanges in other fields, officially denied from time to time, throughout the first half of the decade.

China's attitudes to Israel over the previous decades had more in common with those prevalent in Arab and Moslem countries than with the Communist bloc. The latter had maintained diplomatic and commercial relations with Israel for extended periods, unlike China. But China's policies and world view underwent radical change in the post-Cultural Revolution period. Economic modernization became the primary policy goal, and the task of China's foreign policy was to serve modernization and the concomitant 'opening to the outside world'. These changes in national policies and international perspective brought an end to China's 'treatment of Israel as a non-country'[2] and made possible the secret contacts and exchanges of the early 1980s. The four years following this first meeting of their Foreign Ministers at the General Assembly in 1987 were to bring the two countries to the threshold of full diplomatic relations.

The following pages are a personal account of the development of covert official contacts and exchanges in Beijing, commencing with the author's arrival, early in March 1991, as Special Adviser at the Beijing Liaison Office of the Israel Academy of Sciences and Humanities, and concluding with the establishment of diplomatic relations in January 1992. This office had been established during 1990, following agreement between the Foreign Ministers in autumn 1989, at what had become their annual General Assembly meeting. Non-governmental offices were to be set up in the two countries, on the Chinese side a branch of the China International Tourist Service in Israel, and the above-mentioned Israel office in Beijing, which was formally opened in June 1990.

At the September 1990 meeting of the Foreign Ministers at the General Assembly session in New York, Israel's Deputy Prime Minister and Foreign Minister, David Levy, proposed sending 'one of our senior Ambassadors' to the Beijing Liaison Office, in order that the potential dialogue between the two countries be developed and conducted on a more regular basis, in Beijing. The Chinese

2. Julian M. Sobin, 'The China–Israel Connection: New Motivations for Rapprochement', *The Fletcher Forum of World Affairs*, 15, 1, Winter 1991, p. 11.

response was positive, and after some months of patience and preparation, we were informed early in 1991 that a visa would be issued to me at the consular section of the Chinese Embassy in London. My task was to further the development of discreet political and official exchanges, in addition to the academic and agricultural exchanges, which had been the mandate of the Liaison Office.

China's assent to the addition of this political dimension to the Office's functions, and of a senior Foreign Service officer to the staff, so soon after its establishment the previous year, was significant and promising for the further development of contacts and relations. So began the third stage of the slow and gradual progress towards normalization of relations between two countries, which had never maintained official relations. Contacts of various kinds, particularly between the military establishments of the two countries, in the aftermath of the 1979 China–Vietnam border clashes, had been reported in the press throughout the early and mid-1980s, at times illustrated with photographs of what was purported to be Israeli artillery mounted on Chinese tanks in Beijing's annual military parades. These press reports were met with official denials, from both sides. This could be defined as the first stage of highly discreet exchanges, arising out of national interest on both sides, as well as from the changes in China's post-Cultural Revolution world view.

The second stage may be traced not only to the first meetings of the Foreign Ministers at UN General Assembly sessions, but also to discreet contacts elsewhere. Those between Israel's Consul General and the Head of the New China News Agency bureau in Hong Kong laid the groundwork for the Ministers' meetings and for the subsequent establishment of the non-governmental offices, that of the China International Travel Service in Tel Aviv and of the Israel Academy of Sciences and Humanities in Beijing.

The third and final stage, of direct, if still clandestine, political and official exchanges between Beijing and Jerusalem, and between the two Foreign Ministries, was about to begin. This was the stage which would lead to the establishment of diplomatic relations. The question was how prolonged and gradual this stage would prove to be, and how many years it might take to blossom into full and open relations, given Chinese patience and inclination to proceed step by step (*yibu yibu*), with the utmost circumspection.

1

Beijing initiation

EARLY MARCH is not the best time of the year to arrive in Beijing. The atmosphere is damp and chilling, and the skies tend to be grim and overcast. The use of coal to heat several million homes, offices and factories throughout the winter creates a gigantic cloud or accumulation of semi-condensed smoke overhead, irrigated and thickened with the damp of the early spring. This envelops the hills to the west and north which, at kindlier seasons of the year, lend to the flat city sprawl an attractive, scenic background.

There are few evergreens in the city, and the soft and cheerful blossom, flowers and foliage which abound along every city road-way and highway at other seasons are still in harsh hibernation. The towering office and residential blocks and the wide avenues criss-crossing the city look bare and drab, unappealing and cold to the newcomer. The first impression is of an ant-hill of a city. People are ubiquitous. The Chinese are an outdoor people, and at this time of the year, they move more quickly in the cold than in the warmer seasons. The several layers of clothing, which traditionally serve Chinese as protection from the rigours of winter, give an appearance of drabness and uniformity, in contrast to the light, varied and colourful garb, particularly that of the children and the younger folk, in other seasons.

In the spring of 1991, vitality and prosperity were the newcomer's first impression. Gross National Product was growing at an annual rate of 7 per cent nationally, much higher in the cities. The fulfilment of Chinese aspirations for material well-being, 'clothing, a roof over your head, food and wheels under your feet', i.e. a bicycle or cart, (*yi, shi, zhu, xing*), was very much in evidence. Every street was a lively market. Over 60 per cent of farm produce was already being privately marketed in 1991, much of it by the farmers and their families at their own street stalls. People were visibly well fed and clothed. The abundantly stocked and busy food shops and clothing stalls were manifest evidence of material prosperity. The black canvas, rubber-soled slippers, in which all and sundry had been shod up till only a year or two previously, were being rapidly replaced with western-style leather shoes, made in China and exported on a vast scale. The man in the street could and did respond to festive or Spring Festival greetings with the tag 'every day is a festive day'. This was not a commonly used expression, and the Chinese language tutor who told me about it may have merely been seeking a way to express to the foreigner his pride in the new China, of plenty and stability. But after so prolonged a period of deprivation, suffering and instability, in which the mass famine of 1960–61, when 20 to 30 million Chinese are estimated to have died of hunger was followed by the harsh and bitter conditions of the Cultural Revolution decade, every day now brought its bountiful food, clothing and family joys, rather than the public and private distress and afflictions of the past.

This was a China well on its way to achieving the quadrupling of its GNP in the last two decades of the century, the target set by elder statesman Deng Xiaoping and the party leadership at the Twelfth Party Congress, in 1982. Far from post-Tiananmen China relapsing into a more rigid and closed society, or reverting to 'the grim cycle of protest and repression'[1], the scene greeting the newcomer to Beijing in early spring, 1991, was that of a dynamic economy, growing exposure to market forces and an openness, which could by no means be defined in exclusively economic terms. To what extent this situation and general atmosphere might facilitate contacts with official Beijing for an Israel Foreign Ministry emissary, newly seconded to the Beijing Liaison Office of the Israel Academy of Sciences and Humanities, remained to be explored.

The learning process in so novel an environment begins at first contact. The two youngsters in military uniform at airport border control were obviously confused, not only by the unfamiliarity of

---

1. Jonathan D. Spence, *The Search for Modern China* (London: Hutchinson, 1990), pp.624–6.

the Israeli passport and its Hebrew markings, but more so with the fact that the passport was back to front, if not upside down. In my first Chinese sentence uttered on China's soil, I explained to them that I was from Israel, that the strange script on the passport was Hebrew, which runs from right to left, and the passport, therefore, was to be opened from right to left. But it was not this utterly weird, foreign devil's incongruities, which engaged their interest. The mention of Israel elicited spontaneous, enchanting Chinese smiles, lighting up their young faces. 'Israel strong, Israel powerful, Israel self-reliant', they chimed at me, self-reliance (*dz li*) being a highly respected, Maoist attribute, featuring in Chinese clichés and popular sayings.

It was a revealing first encounter. These two young men could only have known of Israel from what they constantly read and heard in the Chinese media about the 'Zionist entity' and its criminal acts of aggression against its Arab neighbours, its cruel oppression of the Palestinians, whose lands it had occupied, and its subservience to the Western imperialists and their interests. Yet, from the indoctrination and constant anti-Israeli propaganda, they had drawn their own conclusions, based on their instinctive common sense. As one Chinese friend later explained to me, they were confronted with the map of the Middle East and the vast Arab lands encircling Israel in the television newscasts or on the pages of the *People's Daily*, in the reports of Israel's latest wrong-doings. What was clear to them was that little Israel could handle the Moslem hordes and hold her own against the vast, oil-rich Arab hinterland. This image earned their respect, not hostility. The Chinese people were accustomed to reading between the lines and making their own evaluations of what was served up to them by the official media. I was to encounter almost invariably in my contacts with Chinese people, themselves confronted with an Israeli for the first time in their lives, this same positive and enthusiastic first reaction, as evinced by the two young paramilitary at Beijing's Shoudu (Capital) Airport.

There was another significant lesson to be learned from this first encounter. These two young Chinese offered the warmest and friendliest of welcomes to the Israeli visitor, without fear of each other or apprehension of deviating from a dictated consensus or official orthodoxy of antagonism, if not hostility towards Israel.

I had landed in the post-Mao China, of the 'second revolution' and the era of Deng Xiaoping, with its own, broadened parameters of freedom of thought and expression.

I embarked upon my first round of calls in Beijing not, as is the case with Ambassadors, according to a formally prescribed list. These formal calls, on official personages as well as fellow-Ambassadors, occupy the early weeks and months of the sojourn of an Ambassador in a new posting. They enable him to become acquainted with appropriate people, who can be consulted and advise him thereafter on many of the matters of his daily work agenda. He will meet these same people constantly, at official ceremonies and receptions, and they constitute a kind of informal professional guild, of which he is automatically a member.

My own position was quite different. I had no position or status in the diplomatic and official community. I was expected by the host government to maintain a low profile, as adviser to an academic office, and not to intrude openly upon the official diplomatic scene, of which I was not intended to be part. Ambassadors in Beijing whom I knew from other postings, or who had been informed of my arrival by mutual friends and colleagues, were aware of the reservations of the host government concerning my particular status. This may have inhibited them in their contacts with me. On the other hand, the arrangements under which I had come to Beijing did give me access to the Foreign Ministry, limited, at the outset, to its West Asian and North African Department.

For a foreigner, venturing out for the first time onto the wide avenues and teeming side-streets of the Beijing megalopolis, with its 10 million inhabitants and million or more bicycles, two- and three-wheel carts, trucks, cabs and private vehicles, his Chinese chauffeur plays a key role. Knowledge of English is a rare, and therefore valuable commodity in China, even amongst the service personnel assigned to foreign businesses and homes. Foreigners are not allowed to hire help, except through the official employment agencies for foreigners. The Ministry of Foreign Affairs has its own service bureau, supplying all local personnel required by Embassies and diplomatic households. The personnel are, in fact, Foreign Ministry employees. When diplomatic relations were eventually established and our office became an Embassy, the two senior local employees assigned to us, in response to our request for reliable local staff, had recently returned from junior diplomatic postings at China's Embassies in Baghdad and Cairo. They were invaluable in guiding us through the mazes of official Beijing and its bureaucracies, and they were as personable as they were experienced and helpful.

The Foreign Ministry's Diplomatic Service Bureau concludes employment contracts with the Embassies and receives the local employees' salaries. This is not only a system of control, but also a source of income for the Ministry, which passes on to the employee as little as one half of the salary payment. However, it makes available to the employee the services and social benefits provided by governmental and state-owned enterprises to staff and their families, medical, education and even housing. In addition, the employee usually receives agreed extra payments directly from the foreign employer, and these alone can be far higher than the average salary in equivalent employment in the local sector.

Our domestic employees were provided at this stage by a government agency, catering to foreign businesses. Neither driver nor cook spoke English. Otherwise, they would have been in even better-paid work. Setting forth on my first round of calls, I gave my driver his instructions and he proceeded to compliment me on my Chinese, even on my tones (there are four tones in Mandarin, each of which entirely alters the meaning of a word). Had I been wary rather than flattered, I might have realized that there was further need to make myself clear. I was delivered to the wrong address. My driver would never tell me that he had not understood my Chinese. It would have caused both of us embarrassment and loss of face. The civilized atmosphere and the rules of mutual exchanges and relationship between driver and foreign employer were far more important than reaching somewhere at a given time. In this way, I learned that polite reactions require careful, appropriate interpretation, and I repeated my instructions employing all the Chinese synonyms I could muster, until I could be sure that my four tones were, indeed, clear and distinct. Only then did we reach our first destination. To be late in China is to be ill-mannered. The Chinese are forever making allowances for foreigners' behaviour, but that did not make my hosts at the New China News Agency headquarters happy with the fact that I had apparently not considered this first meeting with them important enough to set off in good time and arrive, if anything, early. Only when I told them the story of my Chinese and the driver did they relax and relent.

A day or two after my arrival, the first dinner of welcome was tendered in my honour, significantly by the Chinese Academy of Sciences, the host organization of the Liaison Office of the Israeli Academy. This was a clear message concerning the nature of my own formal accreditation. However, within a week of my arrival I did find myself in the Foreign Ministry meeting rooms. These are the Chinese equivalent of faded Dickensian parlours, with their heavy, old-fashioned, plush armchairs from another day and age, as were the enormous chandeliers and heavy, brocade drapes. I was received courteously, even warmly, first by the Deputy Head of Department, a few days later by the Head of Department, and about a week after that by the Deputy Minister responsible for our region. He reminded me that 'the Foreign Ministry is now the address for raising bilateral, political matters and activities, and we ask you not to take these elsewhere, not to go to others, here, with political matters.'

This was clearly intended as guidance for my activities and their range at the outset, as well as what sounded like an expression of inquietude, at the very least, at my direct approaches to a variety of semi-official contacts, in the media and public institutions, and perhaps even at the contents of my first meetings and discussions with these new contacts. At the same time, it constituted official verification of my role as a political officer, representing the Israeli government and responsible for conducting the dialogue and exchanges with the Chinese Foreign Ministry. Nevertheless, it was necessary to explore the possibilities and contacts available to me outside the Ministry, as well as their limitations. These were mainly with the official, governmental New China News Agency, Xinhua, as mentioned earlier, and the daily press, which can be a power unto itself, even in China. Similarly, the *People's Daily* is, from time to time, a centre of power within the regime and the Communist Party. In addition, official foreign affairs research and information gathering institutions serve government at all levels in Beijing. Some of these are direct channels to the leadership. Their personnel tend to be interested in developing contacts with the foreign community, and the reverse is certainly true. My colleagues and I developed good contacts in these directions at the earliest stage of our presence in Beijing. Being quasi-academic, they were entirely legitimate targets for our attentions and overtures. For their part, they appeared to be neither inhibited nor constrained in their responsiveness.

The next major step forward in the new, official dialogue between the two Ministries of Foreign Affairs was already in the works. A key guiding rule in our mutual contacts, constantly reiterated to me by our Chinese hosts, was a kind of speed limit on the momentum of their development. It was *yibu yibu*, or 'step by step', an earlier mentioned precept of which our hosts in the Foreign Ministry would remind me, whenever they felt that I was pressing a little too hard on the accelerator. The next step was their agreement to a secret visit to Beijing on the part of Israeli Foreign Ministry Director General Reuven Merhav. He had initiated the renewed political contacts after 1986, with the New China News Agency bureau in Hong Kong, where he was then posted as Consul General. He guided and accompanied the process which had led to the opening of the Liaison Office in Beijing and, now, to the initiation of my role within its framework.

The visit was scheduled for the latter part of March, a few weeks after my arrival. This would be the first visit of an Israeli Foreign Ministry functionary to be hosted, however clandestinely, by the Chinese Foreign Ministry. My colleagues and I at the Liaison Office were restricted to service passports, at the Chinese request. This was the first occasion in over 30 years that the bearer of an Israeli diplomatic passport was issued an official entry visa to China, as opposed to the tourist or group visas, issued in the case of previous secret or private visits of Israeli officials, as well as to Israeli tourist groups, to which entry had first been permitted about a year earlier.

On 14 March 1991, about a week before Merhav's planned arrival, the Israeli English-language daily, the *Jerusalem Post* carried a headline, 'Merhav to hold talks in Beijing'. The report stated that he would hold talks with Foreign Minister Qian Qichen. An article on an inside page of the same issue of the newspaper, written by a former Australian junior diplomat in Beijing, now living in Jerusalem, commented on the unfortunate nature of this leak, raising the possibility that it could lead to the cancellation of the visit, 'given the paranoia about relations with Israel in Chinese official circles'. The story was promptly picked up by the Hong Kong press and other international newspapers.

The following day, in the course of my first meeting with members of the editorial staff of Beijing's English-language daily, the *China Daily*, there was an urgent telephone message from the Liaison Office to the effect that my younger colleague and assistant, Yoel Guilatt, was summoned urgently to a meeting with the Assistant Director of the West Asian and North African Department of the Foreign Ministry. There was some little drama in our on-the-spot discussion, in the presence of our *China Daily* hosts, in which we decided that he should leave the meeting, with apologies to our hosts, and go straight to the Foreign Ministry. In the following weeks, we had regular meetings with some of those same staff members of the *China Daily*, but never did any of them so much as mention the urgent summons, let alone seek to elicit information about it. If they were at all surprised at the very fact of our contacts with the Foreign Ministry, they certainly gave no sign of it. One could rely upon the discretion of Chinese journalists in such circumstances, as well as upon their sense of professional responsibility and good judgement. The myriad Chinese sayings and maxims are, in many cases, precepts for proper behaviour. One of these is 'what should not be spoken do not speak, what should not be heard, do not hear, what should not be asked, do not ask, what should not be seen do not see'.

Guilatt sped off to the Foreign Ministry building, where he was told that the Ministry was offended by the leak to the press in Jerusalem. They had worked very hard in the department to arrange the visit (i.e. to obtain approval from above for their recommendation), and to implement this considerable next step forward in the development of official contacts. As a result of the publicity, it had been contended that the visit should now be postponed. However, after lengthy deliberations the final decision was to go ahead with it. This was the first of many such future exchanges with our Chinese colleagues, in which they were to express dismay and disappointment at leaks to the press in Jerusalem, on matters which had been discussed with us confidentially, particularly in cases of secret visits.

The Chinese were not yet ready for open contacts with Israel. It was essential, therefore, that we be able to develop discreet exchanges. The rules of the game, from their point of view, were gradual development and deepening of the dialogue and ties, under conditions of complete confidentiality, i.e. secrecy. They wished neither to invite nor provoke protestations and interventions from their Arab friends. It was clear to me, at this point, that the Foreign Ministry had been given the green light to develop contacts with us on the above basis, even to proceed towards normalization, gradually, step by step, with the timing, tied to developments in the Middle East itself, being of the essence. From the reactions in the department to the press leaks in Jerusalem, it was my feeling that they were also anxious to avoid second thoughts at the higher, decision-making levels, or reconsideration of the green light which they had been given, to implement a policy of gradual progress towards normalization of relations with Israel. The challenge could come from the Arab world's old friends in the government and party hierarchies, or from foreign trade authorities alerted or troubled by Arab or Moslem diplomats in Beijing, or directly from the Arab countries. Breaches of the rules of the game, from their viewpoint, and leaks to the international media could only serve to alert parties interested in challenging or questioning this third and crucial stage of our bilateral contacts. They were never able to understand how and why so much was leaked to the press in Jerusalem, regardless of the potential damage to our mutual efforts, and an unspoken assumption that this could only be deliberate policy on Jerusalem's part was often felt.

On this occasion, the only help and guidance from my own Ministry in Jerusalem came in the form of the Foreign Ministry spokesman's response to reporters' questions: 'The Foreign Ministry Spokesman's comments are confined to the Director General's visit to the Soviet Union and do not refer to the further itinerary. With reference to the rumours on the subject, the Foreign Ministry does not comment on press reports.' This enlightenment from Jerusalem, more suggestive than dismissive, was singularly unhelpful to us. It would have been merely tactless to quote it to our contacts in the West Asian and North African Department.

A few days before Merhav's arrival, I had a meeting with the Head of Department. I made use of the occasion to express regrets at the press reports of the impending visit, coupled with the hope that the mutual confidence so necessary to our joint task of nursing and nurturing the developing contacts between our two countries would remain unimpaired. He responded that his deputy had raised the matter earlier, with Guilatt, and he was not intending to raise it with me. This was not an intimation that the matter was of lesser significance, to be raised on a lower level, but rather that it was so irritating and disagreeable, in addition to the threat it had posed to the visit taking place, that it had been decided to raise it not at the most senior level, so as to minimize the personal embarrassment between him and myself, and certainly not to revert to it unnecessarily at this stage. This was one of many lessons I was to receive in Chinese delicacy and tact. These did not, of course, inhibit the hosts from raising matters of appropriate importance, however disagreeable they might prove to be, at the highest level, whenever it was deemed necessary.

The atmosphere of these early meetings in the department was as courteous and friendly as it was professional. The smiles with which we were received by our hosts were nothing if not welcoming. There are many Chinese smiles, as eloquent and, at times, more so than the verbal ceremonies of welcome and formulas of courtesy preceding the substantial discussion and agenda. Smiles serve most occasions and communicate a wide range of attitudes and reactions in China, if one is experienced and skilled enough in their interpretation. A grave mien and grimaces are not essential to communicate disagreement or displeasure. Even if the foreigner working in China cannot pick up basic Chinese, he needs to distinguish the subtle variation of smiles and laughs, and to learn to interpret some of them. At first encounters, there are the smiles of welcome, rejection or reservation, and of uncertainty. I found it much more agreeable to be put off with a smile, rather than a glare or glance of remonstrance or rejection, when presenting myself to a Chinese who had doubts or qualms about contacts with an Israeli.

Added to the courtesy which is natural to the Chinese were genuine interest and curiosity about this new species of foreigner, from Israel. The Chinese are a curious people, highly alert and interested in what is going on around them, particularly in the unusual and the strange. Most of the people encountered by us had some connection with China's relations with the Middle East. Many had experience of the Arab world, and most of the personnel of the West Asian and North African Department had pursued their entire careers in the Middle East, or dealing with its affairs. They spoke Arabic, as their second language, and only very rarely English. What characterized these people in their contacts with us was their interest in representatives of a country so closely bound up with their professional work and careers, and yet previously so completely 'out of bounds' for them. In addition, we felt a real commitment, if not a vested interest on the part of those who welcomed contacts with us, in the task of promoting mutual relations, upon which we were together embarked.

In the early meetings in the Department, the main item on our agenda was the Gulf War, its implications for future stability in the Middle East and for the prospects of a peace process and problem solving between Israel and her neighbours. China's positions on measures and sanctions against Iraq, and in Security Council discussions, were of interest and concern to us. None of us predicted or surmized the effect the Gulf War was to have on Arafat and his Palestine Liberation Organization (PLO), or that his support for Iraq would cost him so dearly in Arab backing that he would consequently be impelled towards a peace process with Israel and compromise of his own role and profile in the process, at least at the outset.

The Chinese were highly critical of Iraq's aggression against Kuwait, and they told us that they had kept the PLO Ambassador to Beijing constantly informed of their dissatisfaction with PLO support for Iraq. But they were not supportive of western military intervention. They had supported UN Security Council resolutions imposing sanctions but abstained on Resolution 678, permitting the use of armed force against Iraq. Their abstention and, indeed, strong reservations on the use of armed force sprang from their apprehensions concerning what the Chinese called US 'hegemonism' and Soviet 'revisionism', combining, in this case, to create a new order in the region. My own assessment of their position was that they were equally anxious at potential damage to their commercial interests, and to their construction work in a region in which Chinese labourers and workers numbered tens of thousands. In the event, these work forces had to be brought home to China, and they left behind very considerable, outstanding debts to China, which it was to take many years to recover, and only then partially.

However, the more immediate item of discussion at these early meetings was the agenda for the visit of Director General Merhav. This was to be the first step in the exchange of official and secret visits of Chinese and Israeli Foreign Ministry personnel in the two capitals, building up to the level of vice-ministerial and ministerial visits, and with these to full normalization of relations. It was to be the first opportunity, since the January 1955 Israeli delegation's visit to Beijing, to hold thorough and comprehensive exchanges, over a four-day period, as opposed to the previous brief and infrequent encounters in New York and Hong Kong. The Director of the China International Tourist Service (CITS) office in Tel Aviv was a Chinese Foreign Service officer, who had served elsewhere in the Middle East, and one of his assistants was the first Hebrew-speaking Chinese Foreign Service officer. The visit of Merhav as guest of the Chinese Foreign Ministry was to lead to regular contacts on political matters and exchanges of views between these CITS personnel in Israel and the Foreign Ministry in Jerusalem, parallel to our own contacts in Beijing.

Our assessment, on the eve of the visit, was that our hosts viewed the visit itself as a major step forward in our mutual contacts, and that we should not expect to hear from them concrete proposals for additional measures or for changes for the better in the unofficial status of the two offices. The latter was always at the forefront of our minds. Our day-by-day activities in Beijing were formally the promotion and deepening of cultural, scientific and agricultural exchanges and visits. But in tandem with the routinization of these our aim was now to create a routine of official, political exchanges and visits, which would in themselves become equivalent to regular relations and lead to their formal normalization, i.e. the establishment of diplomatic relations.

2

The first leap forward

O N A COLD, sunny spring morning in late March, we drove out
to Capital Airport, directly to the discretely separate area of
the VIP lounges. The Israeli staff members, including our Consul
from Hong Kong, whose participation in the visit had been agreed
upon with our Chinese hosts (and who was later to be transferred
to Beijing and to become Counsellor at our Embassy, upon its
establishment), were greeted in the lounge by West Asian and North
African Department personnel and the Deputy Director. We were
to await the arrivals not on the open tarmac, as is usual with high-
level official visits, nor in full public view at the airport arrival gates,
but in the seclusion of the VIP lounge. Our hosts were not yet ready
for public exposure in our company.

But they were visibly as excited as we by the occasion, and by
what it meant for themselves, as the officials responsible for admini-
stering China's Middle East policies and relations. On this, as on so
many such occasions, we felt part of a joint venture with our Chinese
Foreign Ministry colleagues, the culmination of which would be the
achievement of the mutual goal of diplomatic relations.

One might have expected the welcome to be marked, on the part
of the hosts, by courteous reserve at this first, formal and direct contact
with senior Foreign Ministry officials of a country from which they
had been so completely estranged over the decades. This was not
the case. Chinese hospitality is characterized first and foremost by
a warmth, which is much more readily felt than described. It is
atmospheric, rather than physical and back-slapping. Body language
does come into play in China. But it is facial expression that the
Chinese have developed into an art of communication. On earlier

occasions of contact with unfriendly Chinese representatives in other parts of the world, wooden expressions and cold, fish-like eyes have eloquently communicated disapproval and dismissal, of a kind which I was never to encounter during my stay in China, in this new era of contacts.

The warmth, even heartiness of the welcome on this occasion may have been a little more emphatic than intended, in order to compensate for the lack of common language. Even the formal welcome, seated, ceremoniously and in proper order, in the customary semi-circle in the VIP lounge, had to be filtered through an interpreter, as on all such occasions in China. This affords more time to consider and weigh up what exactly is being said, and in what spirit. On this occasion, the heart of the communication was a clear message of welcome to China, and of looking forward to getting to know each other better.

The Israeli visitors were accommodated in the government guest house, the Diaoyutai (literally 'Fishing Platform'), in a west central suburb of the city, where high ranking, official foreign guests are accommodated. It is a large estate, with about 20 mini-hotels or club-houses, separated by gardens, lakes, bridges and hillocks, in a typically Chinese, landscaped setting. Each mini-hotel has suites and other sleeping accommodation for the VIP and his official staff, as well as its own dining rooms, meeting rooms and reception halls, spacious and beautifully laid out in traditional Chinese styles, with pastoral views and verandas leading out onto the gardens and lakesides. Official working sessions, dinners, audiences and meetings, even press conferences with the foreign visitors are usually held in various buildings on the estate. It is well guarded, and comings and goings are carefully controlled. A diplomatic or official government vehicle is waved in, without checks or delays, and with smart salutes from the military guards.

Our delegation, consisting of Director General Merhav, his aide from Jerusalem and our Consul from Hong Kong, were appropriately impressed with the hospitality and unique environment. We strolled together down the tree-lined paths and across the bridges spanning the small lakes, admiring the architecture and man-made landscape, so typical of Chinese scenic aesthetics, and trying to absorb the fact that there we actually were, Israeli officials behind the bamboo curtain. For us, the Beijing staff, finding ourselves inside the Diaoyutai was another 'first', or breakthrough into official China, as, of course, was the visit itself.

The afternoon of the arrival, after the long, overnight flight from Copenhagen for Merhav and his aide, was passed at the Forbidden City, accompanied by West Asian and North African Department staff members. Overwhelming as a first visit to the Forbidden City cannot but be, the constant realization and awareness of the uniqueness of this first occasion, after 35 years of estrangement, of an official Israeli Foreign Ministry delegation being escorted through the heart of Beijing, as guests of the People's Republic of China's Foreign Ministry, was moving and exciting. Despite the language barriers, or, perhaps, because of them, there was a conviviality, a camaraderie in the relations and contacts between hosts and guests, with our hosts clearly sharing our enthusiasm and excitement. Whenever one of the Israelis in our group heard something novel from one of our Chinese hosts concerning his previous experience in the Middle East – 'when I was serving in Damascus, we used to visit the Golan Heights and look down, admiringly, at your farms and agriculture in the Upper Galilee', or 'I was in Tel Aviv in 1987, accompanying a secret mission' – he would hurry off to one of his colleagues in our group, to share the revelation. Such was the unusual atmosphere of what is normally a routine part of the programme of every official visit to Beijing, touring the Forbidden City with the official hosts, as we were to do on many occasions in the following years.

The first working session was held in a conference room at the Diaoyutai the following morning. The Chinese side was headed by the Director of the Department of West Asian and North African Affairs. The comprehensive discussions on the Middle East situation and the Arab–Israeli dispute provided for the first time an opportunity for both sides to familiarize themselves with the full and detailed positions of the other. The historic background to Israel's anxieties and experience with her Arab neighbours could not have been fully familiar to Chinese Foreign Service officers, who had been consistently exposed to only one side of the story. Yet, they gave the impression of being not unacquainted with the history of Moslem and Arab attitudes to Jews throughout the ages, and with the roots of the Palestine problem. One of them, after listening to our presentations, stressed the fact that their entire careers had been involved with learning about the Arab world, Islam and the Palestine problem.

One could sense a certain uncharacteristic Chinese impatience with our detailed expositions of history and background. Their own response was a kind of pragmatic reaction of let's get back to the here and now, and not be mesmerized by the past. It reflected Dengist realism. They proceeded to present, as expected, their own most recent, comprehensive formulation of Chinese policy on the Palestine problem, namely, Premier Li Peng's five points of 5 October 1989.[1] These had been declaimed by a Chinese Foreign Ministry spokesman at the weekly news briefing only the previous week, in response to a 'fortuitous' question. This was clearly intended to allay Arab anxieties at the press reports of the Merhav visit, as well as to signal to us that China remained faithful to her consistent policy of recent years, and that this policy and its implementation were to be the agenda for discussions, as far as our hosts were concerned.

The five points of China's policy on the Palestine problem, usually – and significantly – referred to in official Chinese statements as 'The Middle East Problem', were advocacy of a political settlement, with all partners refraining from the use of military force; the convening of an international peace conference, under UN auspices, with the participation of the five permanent members of the Security Council and other parties concerned being the preferred method for pursuing negotiations for such a settlement, thereby ensuring China's participation, as a Security Council permanent member. The third point of China's policy, however, allowed for any dialogue acceptable by all parties, including direct dialogue between the PLO and Israel. The fourth point was a call to Israel to cease her suppression of the Palestinian people in the occupied territories and withdraw her troops from these territories, coupled with the position that Israel's security should be ensured; and the final point stated the need for the states of Palestine and Israel to recognize each other and for their peoples to co-exist in peace.

These principles were presented as China's policy formulation at the time of the first visit of Yasser Arafat to Beijing as 'President of

---

1. 'Li Suggests Five Steps for Middle East Peace', *China Daily*, 6 October 1989, p. 1.

The State of Palestine' in 1989, after its establishment had been announced by Arafat at the end of 1988 and China had granted it recognition. They summarized China's policy on what has always been viewed by Beijing as the core of the Middle East problem. At different periods, there have been different stresses, particularly during the Cultural Revolution, when the PLO enjoyed training facilities in China, some logistical support, and received Chinese small arms and other weapons.

China was at that time committed to 'national liberation movements' and 'the armed struggle', as well as manoeuvring to out-bid Soviet 'revisionism'. Its support for the PLO was to be viewed in this context. At the time, China opposed outside intervention in the Middle East, including the international conference idea. Much of this changed with the end of the Cultural Revolution, particularly support for armed struggles, and China began to envisage an international role for itself as a responsible, permanent member of the Security Council.

Premier Li Peng has been considered to be close to the Arab world, as well as being cautious and conservative in the face of proposals for policy changes. The five points of his formulation clearly included the element of Israel's independence and security, as well as a pragmatic attitude to possible alternative channels of dialogue, rather than the exclusivity of UN auspices, which had been a firm fixture of China's policy since the early 1980s. This new formulation was later to be reflected in China's positive and supportive positions on the Madrid Conference, convened at the end of October 1991, and throughout the ensuing process which led up to the channel of secret, direct dialogue in Oslo, during 1993, totally unexpected but warmly welcomed in Beijing.

During over four hours of discussions on the first day of the Merhav visit, all the topics of mutual concern were raised. In addition to the Arab–Israel dispute and its background, we raised the issue of arms sales to the region, particularly missiles and nuclear technology. These, we argued, could serve only as destabilizing factors, encouraging aggressive policies rather than peace processes and threatening Israel's security. Our hosts presented their standard responses on these matters, that over 90 per cent of the weapons reaching the region came from the four other permanent members of the Security Council. China's role as an arms supplier was responsible, as well as marginal, they asserted, and Chinese weapons were intended solely to enhance the defensive capacities of the purchasing states, without affecting the balance of armaments and power in the region. Nor do they constitute a form of intervention in the internal affairs of the recipient states or the region, as is the case with other supplier states. Finally, China has always supported the position that the Middle East should be free of weapons of mass destruction.

With regards to North Korean arms sales to the region, the dangers and implications of which we raised, our hosts responded that the Democratic People's Republic of Korea (DPRK) was a sovereign state pursuing its own policies, in which China does not intervene. Our hosts raised the issue of contacts with Taiwan, always a special area of sensitivity for China, and they were assured of Israel's commitment to the 'One China' policy, adopted 41 years ago, when Israel recognized the People's Republic. We assured our hosts that the only contacts between Israel and Taiwan were of a commercial and non-governmental nature.

The discussions and dinner meetings with the Department were followed, on the final day of the visit, by a two-and-a-half hour meeting with Vice Foreign Minister Yang Fuchang, whose area of responsibility covered the Middle East. Vice Minister Yang was the most senior Foreign Ministry official involved in implementing Middle East policy and perhaps the most experienced in the affairs of the region. Although he had been in Moscow early in his career, in the 1950s, and was a Russian-speaker, he had specialized in the Middle East thereafter, working mainly in the region itself, where he had latterly been Ambassador to Kuwait (appointed Ambassador to Cairo early in 1994), and serving at various levels in the West Asian and North African Department. He spoke Arabic fluently. It was our impression that he was one of the principal architects of the new, incipient relationship and contacts with Israel, on the official level.

The Vice Minister stressed the need for direct dialogue between Israel and the PLO. In fact, in his own summary of Chinese policy in the region, he did not mention the international peace conference idea but dwelt on the essentiality of negotiations between the parties to the dispute, the PLO being 'the sole representative of the Palestinians', without whom there could be no solution. This formulation displayed the ambiguity, or, as the Chinese might have termed it, contradiction, between their support for UN auspices, dating from the early 1980s, with the involvement of the Security Council's permanent members, and their consistent position of longer standing against big power intervention in regional disputes, and in favour of the principle of parties to disputes seeking solutions through direct dialogue and negotiations. But the bottom line was that China's sole interest in the Middle East was the achievement of peace and stability, with the fairness and justice which she had advocated in the Gulf crisis. The reference was to the familiar terminology of 'a fair and just solution' for the Palestinians.

On the bilateral level, the Vice Minister expressed satisfaction with Israel's consistent support for 'One China', and with the exchanges and level of contacts between China and Israel. He stated that China viewed these contacts favourably, but that their further development would be a process, extending over a period of time, the hope being that favourable developments in the Middle East and in Arab–Israeli relations would make possible the establishment of diplomatic relations between our two countries in the not too distant future. 'When a melon ripens, it falls to the ground in its own time', he told us, quoting an old Chinese saying. His advice was that we deepen our bilateral exchanges and talk less about them in public, 'so as not to invite unfriendly intervention and interference'.

This was another occasion on which we were made aware of the fact that our hosts were constantly looking back over their shoulders at the reactions of their friends in the Arab world, and of the pro-Arab support groups or lobbies in China. They also sought to prepare these in advance and win their assent, or, at least, abstention from public opposition to contacts and exchanges with Israel. Our impression and information was that at every stage of the developing relations with Israel, steps were taken to mollify their Arab friends and to persuade them that China–Israel contacts would work only in favour of a fair and just settlement of the Middle East problem, and that China continued to adhere to her consistent support for fair and just Arab aspirations.

With regard to bilateral contacts and exchanges, the Vice Minister reiterated that the two offices, in Tel Aviv and Beijing, should serve, henceforth, as the main channel for bilateral communication and that all political matters should be transmitted and handled through these two offices and the respective Foreign Ministries. Here again, it sounded as though he was also signalling to us not to hawk our political wares elsewhere in Beijing; but this was not made entirely clear, and we continued to feel that we must pursue the path of careful and discreet trial and error, in expanding the range of our official, local contacts.

In conclusion, the Vice Minister described the visit as an important development in bilateral official exchanges, and he stressed the aspect of secrecy, expressing regret at its necessity at this stage. He added that he looked forward to further visits of this kind. He referred to the press leaks of the visit, and he told us that the Foreign Ministry spokesman would be answering a question at the weekly press briefing that day. He would confirm that there had been such a visit, but that it was a private visit. There would be no acknowledgement of official contacts or involvement in the visit. At this point, he reiterated their hope that there would be no further publicity or leaks of the contents of the talks, as this could only have undesirable effects.

During the following week, the Israeli press carried several reports of the visit. Headlines read 'Ties with China Expected' (*Jerusalem Post*, 27 March 1991) and 'Relations between Israel and China on way to Normalization' (*Maariv*, 27 March 1991). The contents of the reports attributed to Merhav expressions of optimism concerning the future of relations, and the assumption that China understood the need for official relations with Israel as a prior condition for playing a role in the post-Gulf War Middle East. China's Foreign Minister Qian was asked at a Beijing press conference on 28 March to comment on a report of the Israeli Broadcasting Services, Kol Israel, of the preceding day, attributing to 'a senior Israeli official' predictions of normalization of China–Israel relations in the next few months. The Foreign Minister replied that there were no political ties between China and Israel, and that the recent visit to China of an Israeli official had been in an unofficial capacity. He did mention the existence of the two offices, our Beijing Liaison Office of the Israel Academy, and the CITS tourist office in Tel Aviv.

When our office telephoned the Foreign Ministry Information Department, requesting the official text of the Minister's reply, we were told that they would look into the matter. After waiting an hour or two, we called again. This time, we were referred to the West Asian and North African Department, as if to signal to us that this was still our one and only address in the Ministry. We had a similar experience a week or two later, when my secretary requested a meeting for me with the International Organizations Department, to learn about China's position in the Security Council deliberations of Draft Resolution 681, on the Gulf War. She was given an appointment for me not with that department, but with the Deputy Director of West Asia and North Africa. At the meeting, he was his usual charming and affable self, but unable to provide a detailed briefing and information on specialized aspects outside his jurisdiction and competence. At this stage, we were clearly being confined to our first point of official contact. But we, for our part, had to explore the possibilities of extending contacts, certainly within the Foreign Ministry and the areas of interest and concern to us.

At previous meetings, this Deputy Director had addressed me as 'Ambassador' and 'Excellency', in accordance with my foreign service rank. On this occasion, I was demoted to 'old friend', an amicable and cordial form of address in China, or I was referred to more formally as 'Special Adviser', my official title at our Liaison Office. On future occasions, I was again addressed with the diplomatic appellations, and I could draw whatever conclusions or read whatever significance I wished into the variations. In fact, I came to view them as part of the Chinese mixture of courtesy and cordiality, rather than varying political signals on the level of bilateral diplomacy.

At this time of the year, Premier Li delivered his comprehensive, annual report to the National People's Congress spring session. In it, he urged that with the end of the Gulf War, the Middle East question (i.e. the Arab–Israeli dispute) 'should be placed on the agenda, and an early, just and reasonable solution to the issue should be worked out'. China's own views on the contents of such a solution were presented, in the form of the familiar five points, with one or two embellishments. 'The Chinese government and people have always supported the just cause of the Palestinian and other Arab people', he declared, and the tensions in the occupied territories of

Palestine have been a major concern to the international community. He gave acknowledgement to the 'serious impact of the developments in the Gulf situation on the political settlement of the Middle East question', without going so far as to predict how the weakening of Arafat's PLO, resulting from its identification with Iraq in the Gulf War and loss of support and aid from the rest of the Arab world, might lead to a new readiness to compromise and lend renewed impetus to various forms of negotiations.

Our reading of this statement of policy was that the close contacts and comprehensive exchanges of the previous weeks notwithstanding, there had been no change or softening in the tone of Chinese positions, as far as Palestinian rights and Israel's occupation of territory were concerned. It was the actual visit which was significant, not any illusions that such an initial exchange of views might already have perceptible impact on policy statements.

We were able to elicit some feedback, from well-informed, semi-official contacts outside the Foreign Ministry. The talks were very useful indeed, we were told, as a first opportunity for hearing and presenting positions, fully and comprehensively. Reports had been passed up and down the system and hierarchy. But there had been no surprises, as far as our hosts were concerned, and the differences of opinion and viewpoints remained. We understood from these reports that they saw no need even to review or re-examine policies or nuances at this stage. I asked my best informed and highest placed contact what he thought the prospects might be for a return visit to Israel. His response was revealing. He saw no prospects, at this time, of a Chinese Foreign Ministry delegation to Israel, 'because it could not be kept discreet and confidential'. He might well have said that there was nothing to add at this stage, after the Merhav visit. But he chose to stress how the Chinese side viewed the publicity surrounding the Merhav visit. What followed was to demonstrate further that our hosts viewed the development of relations in terms of actual visits and exchanges of this kind. Therefore, the lack of discretion and confidentiality caused them concern. But in fact, they were already preparing the next step forward, despite the publicity of the previous visit. This, however, is to anticipate, and the following few weeks, before the surprise of the timing of the next step forward, were to pass in a flurry of activities and new experiences.

3

Striking roots

D URING THESE early weeks, it was a novel learning experience to meet, formally and informally, with semi-official contacts from the press, and from political research and other institutions concerned with foreign affairs, and to explore the limits of sociability and confidences, both cross-culturally and in the political environ- ment of Beijing. Some of these contacts carried multiple visiting cards, and at this stage I was privileged to be handed the card denoting the less official function, position or title. In one case, a senior Communist Party functionary gave me his card as committee member of an international friendship association. In another, a State Council official presented himself to me in his role as honorary officer of a cultural exchange institution. Both roles, as presented to me, were, presumably, more suited in the host country's view to contacts with me, in view of my status at the time, rather than the more official roles which, in fact, had led me to seek out these contacts. Several months were to pass before these same officials presented me with visiting cards denoting their official roles. When they did so, it may have been intended to appear haphazard, as though the personages concerned did not remember that they had previously presented cards denoting other roles. But it was surely deliberate and officially co-ordinated.

At this time, I met a foreign academic and business consultant, a Chinese-speaker who had been coming to China regularly, over a decade, as an adviser to government bodies on a variety of inter- national transactions. He had raised with his own contacts the subject of China–Israel relations, even in writing, and he offered to arrange for me to meet with some of them for a chat. I did not hear from him again at the time. He had obviously been unaware of what contacts were permissible in my case, and he must have been warned off by the reactions of his Chinese contacts, when he broached the possibility of their meeting with me. I met him a second time almost two years later, and it was not even felt appropriate to comment on or make any apologies for the earlier failure to follow up. Such situations were assumed to be understood and basic in work and contacts in China, not requiring explanations. But I was constantly asking myself – for lack of anyone else to ask – why I was able to meet and develop good contacts with this or that personage, and whether any of these contacts were really fortuitous and dependent solely on my own initiative.

The exchanges at these encounters could be quite frank, even intimate, especially when interpreters were not needed, and one would talk of families, even gossip about mutual friends. Topics ranged from the politics of China and its leadership to Tiananmen and the Cultural Revolution. This latter was a subject on which many people in China seemed to feel the need to unburden themselves, in the only way possible, by talking about their own experiences of that time. Perhaps they were affirming to themselves, rather than to their foreign interlocutor, that such madness would never be allowed to recur. A former Red Guard would speak of his own role at the time, without any questions of personal guilt or shame.

At this distance in time, all shared in the trauma of that horrendous experience, and none could even try to explain, to themselves or to others, how it came about. All were victims of a communal and national aberration, in the collective and community nature of Chinese life and responsibility. There appeared to be no perception of personal guilt or individual responsibility, on the part of ordinary citizens, for what had happened in their society, apart from the officially designated criminals and the Gang of Four. Nor did one detect in conversation about that period attribution of blame to the regime and political system. Mao had erred, and despite his historic contribution to the Chinese revolution and liberation, he was a mere mortal, not a god, according to a popular saying frequently quoted to explain his errors and fallibility. But to fault Mao in such a way as to question his historic contribution and role would be to question the political system and authority of the party.

The generally accepted verdict appeared to be that all had suffered at that time, and that the arch-criminals had been tried and punished. Although in the years immediately following the end of the rule of the Gang of Four, there were great numbers of Chinese who could never forget or forgive the tormentors of their families and themselves, these feelings of bitterness were not allowed to threaten the new order and stability. As time passed, the Chinese people were united by the collective conclusion and resolve never again to tread that path. This was in the spirit of an old Chinese saying, 'loosen control, and chaos ensues' (*yi fang jyou luan*), which could only serve to strengthen government and its authority.

One group which was 'uncontrolled', as far as my access was concerned, was the foreign community. My mission in China was not with them, but they could be of help and guidance. This was particularly true of the diplomatic corps, less so of the press. The foreign press was almost invariably harshly critical of the regime. It was committed to the west's view of human rights and democracy. Undeterred by concepts of cultural relativism, or simply looking for stories considered newsworthy outside China, they sought out China's dissidents and non-conformists. They did not feel obliged to explain to their readers anything about different cultures or values, or that east is east, not west. Their unquestioned premise was that China's society and government were to be measured and censured by US and western standards, certainly as far as human rights and systems of government were concerned. For most of the foreign journalists I met in Beijing, it was not to be entertained that a code prescribing individual rights and duties in a society, and societal values in general, might differ from that of the western world and still be valid, or 'moral'. Even the 'sinologists', or old China hands amongst them, those who had studied Chinese history, culture and language, tended to measure and evaluate the political scene and government on the basis of their own norms and values, rather than in terms of Chinese culture, tradition and circumstance. Politically, they were still traumatized by Tiananmen, and they were harshly critical of the leadership, its handling of that situation, and of its reassertion of strict societal controls at the time. They seemed to give no thought to the question of whether such controls were part and parcel of Chinese society and history, alien as they may be to some contemporary western traditions, or of the historic dangers of chaos and suffering, war lords and warring states.

As to the brutality of Tiananmen, still reverberating two years later, it may well have been 'oriental' and alien to westerners; but many of my Chinese friends, who were horrified by Tiananmen for their own reasons, found it difficult to understand the depth of western revulsion at the visual brutality of Tiananmen. During these years, they were exposed, themselves, to televised pictures and reports of massacres, mass rapes, starvation and mutilations of civilians perpetrated by Europeans against Europeans, in the former Yugoslavia and regions of the former USSR. These were not accompanied by the same universal, western condemnation and revulsion. On the contrary, it seemed to my Chinese friends that westerners were either taking partisan positions or standing aloof, in the face of the most basic human rights being trampled under foot in their own European heartland. Only on Tiananmen, they would add, had the west presented a united, moral front, without any real understanding of what had happened there.

Premier Li's press conference at the closing National People's Congress session in April illustrated these differences. The western correspondents submitted questions related almost exclusively to Tiananmen, its after-effects (two years later) and human rights, and they phrased their questions in the relatively critical and aggressive tones of press conferences in the west, rather than in the language and tones of information seeking. The Chinese journalists were a complete contrast. Their tone and style were polite, respectful and deferential towards their Prime Minister. The contents of their questions suggested entirely different concerns. They probed into economic policies, with implied criticism of aspects of these policies. Chinese journalists and non-journalists are openly critical of economic performance, of corruption in high places, and even of the growing income gaps and emerging moneyed classes. For the Chinese, the most basic of human rights are food and sustenance, a stable society, and effective government authority and control ensuring food supplies and stability. In his answers to these questions, Premier Li alluded to the disintegration in the USSR and eastern Europe as having been avoided in China, thereby ensuring the stability essential for continued economic development.

In the economic sphere, too, the foreign press corps tended to be critical. They constantly pointed to the absence of laws, or even clear administrative practices and rules governing business, commerce and taxation. In each case, separate negotiations were necessary, without entrepreneurs being in a position to learn in advance official requirements and their own liabilities, and to make their calculations on that basis. The foreign press, like their Chinese colleagues and, indeed, Chinese leaders, were highly critical of the corruption and bribery in the system. There were those who argued that the Chinese were too traditional in their thinking and attitudes to be capable of fashioning a modern, rational market economy and society. Deng, himself, called for liberating the mind from the old, fixed patterns of thought (*jyefang szxiang*). Others criticized the arrogance of the Middle Kingdom, the expectation that the foreign investor or entrepreneur would do all the running and examine even the most unrealistic projects proposed by their Chinese hosts.

The general climate of opinion in the foreign press corps was further influenced, at the time, by Chinese positions in the Security Council debates on measures to protect Kurdish and Shia minorities in Iraq against Iraqi President Saddam Hussein's angry and vengeful troops. China opposes uninvited foreign intervention in another state's internal affairs and problems. In this case, she found herself aligned with Cuba, Zimbabwe, India and Ecuador in the Security Council debate. These belonged to the group of Third World countries, which were becoming more and more isolated, ineffective and irrelevant on the Gulf War issue and its aftermath, as well as on the major international economic problems and problem-solving in general. A pragmatic, forward-looking China was expected to take positions more similar to those of Singapore, Japan and South Korea, rather than India and Cuba. China has found itself in some dilemma, as it seeks to fulfil its traditional role as the leading great power in a disintegrating and irrelevant non-aligned movement and Third World, and in the North–South divide, and at the same time to pursue its own absolute priorities of industrial and technological development and foreign trade expansion. For these, China's opening to the developed world and relations with the West are paramount. Its principled and strategic opposition to 'hegemonism' and foreign interventionism, particularly on the part of the United

States, has to be reconciled with the mutual interest, shared with the west, and even with the hegemonists, of eliminating non-western acts of aggression and damaging disputes and clashes in the Gulf, Cambodia and elsewhere in the Third World. These were some of the wide-ranging views and analyses of China's international positions, which I was hearing from foreign journalists in Beijing.

My own conclusions at this time were that China would gradually improve relations with Israel, not in search of a major international role in Middle East peace-making, but to the extent that China's ability to contribute to a peaceful solution of the Middle East problem would be facilitated thereby. This problem, in China's view, was at the heart of instability, in a region geographically and ethnically close to China's own western provinces, and where there was much business to be done. China of the 'second revolution' and of the 'opening to the outside world' policy was interested in gradual normalization of relations with all those countries which had been excluded by the ideological positions of Mao's China. Such normalization of relations would serve China's economic and technological interests and goals.

I continued making my first contacts with Chinese journalists and editors, and with heads of bureaux of international affairs and political research, which serve various government agencies, including the party leadership and the State Council. These bureaux, like the organizations for international friendship and understanding, and for cultural relations and exchanges, with which we had contacts, were semi-official organs, serving government without being officially listed as government agencies. Their personnel were often recruited from the government departments which they served, in what appeared to be a systematic interchange.

Requests for meetings met with a variety of responses, in which no clear pattern was discernible. Some responded with alacrity, arranged meetings immediately, receiving me with courtesy and at a high level. In institutions with which the Liaison Office had developed previous contacts, I was now received at a higher level. But there were those who failed to return our telephone calls, or made various, polite excuses, with the kind of Chinese tact and charm which left one unsure whether the response was really negative, or an invitation to keep on trying. One prominent institutional personality's secretary told my secretary that her director was not 'the appropriate level' for contacts with our office. Three weeks later, following the Merhav visit, of which he had certainly been informed, he did receive me and subsequently became a regular and useful contact. An odder experience was with a former colleague of the 'appropriate level' personality, at the time serving as head of a foreign affairs related organization. His secretary did not return our call. But nine months later, at a reception I held in honour of visiting Israel Deputy Prime Minister and Foreign Minister David Levy, to mark the establishment of diplomatic relations, in late January 1992, the personality concerned came to the reception and apologized for having been abroad so much during the year that he had been unable to fix a meeting with me. This was not in accord with the old Chinese precept of not saying what need not be said.

It can be assumed that in many such cases, the people approached consulted with the Foreign Ministry's West Asian and North African Department. In most cases, the Ministry's response would most likely have been positive, even to institutions which, for their own reasons, might choose to steer clear of contacts with our office and personnel. Many institutions and organizations had a foreign affairs officer, usually a Party functionary, whose task it was to supervise and control contacts with foreigners. But this did not seem to be the case with institutions dealing with foreign affairs and foreigners, which appeared to have their own ranges of discretion and channels of authority.

One visit in these early weeks illustrated the problem of the vast variety of institutions dealing with foreign policy and international affairs, and the need to distinguish which of these actually influenced decision-making levels. A meeting was arranged for me with the director of an institution associated with a government Ministry, from which it drew most of its budget. Himself a former top-level government employee, he received me in an old, palatial mansion, situated in its own small park. The complex had served as a foreign Embassy in years gone by, when diplomacy was very much more sumptuous and extravagant. His institution consisted of several research divisions, staffed by hundreds of research officers. Apart from the regular flow of studies and papers, they produced a quarterly journal in Chinese and collections of selected articles in

English. My questions related to distribution of their material and feedback, these being indications of influence and impact. They had mailing lists of some six thousand addressees, but, I was told frankly and honestly, feedback ranged from rare to non-existent. In some such institutions, we had learned not only of feedback, but of recipients of their reports questioning their analyses and conclusions. Our task was to allocate our very limited time and resources where these could prove effective, in a government administration served by scores of auxiliary institutions, which were often impenetrable mysteries for the foreigner, if not for the Chinese, themselves.

In the weeks following the Merhav visit, our contacts with the West Asian and North African Department were conducted on two levels, those of the Department Director and of his Deputy. Our agenda was the Middle East peace process, and the current efforts to convene the parties in some form or forum of negotiations, in which the US State Department was the principal initiator and intermediary. Washington DC was keeping Moscow informed and involved. It was clear to us that Beijing was also being kept in the picture. The Chinese were encouraging these moves and urging our co-operation, rather than promoting their own views on international auspices for the forum of negotiations. Their priority was progress towards solution of the dispute, whatever their traditional apprehensions concerning Soviet and United States involvement, intervention or 'hegemonism'. For our part, we sought information at these meetings on China's positions on the complex developments in the aftermath of the Gulf War. The Chinese were more suspicious and critical of the continued intervention in Iraq. Their interest was in repairing the damages of the war, and rehabilitating Kuwait, rather than in the efforts to discipline Iraq and control her production of arms, conventional or otherwise, this being the policy of the western countries.

In the margins of these visits to the Foreign Ministry, we noted the friendly and collegial atmosphere created by our hosts. There was never any delay in fixing appointments, at our request, and we were always made to feel welcome. We also paid attention to such finer points as how far our hosts escorted us from the meeting room to the Ministry front steps and the waiting car, in full view of the comings and goings of other foreign diplomats, visiting the building.

This would vary. In the early weeks, we were not escorted as far as the front steps and waved off, as the car drove away. This would have been 'maximum exposure', and it took a few more weeks until our hosts began to shed their public shyness and emerge with us onto the front steps. The personal relations forged in the course of the next 'leap forward' must surely have contributed to this. But that is to anticipate.

4

A new leap forward

Our CHINESE colleagues in the West Asian and North African Department found it necessary, at this time, to pour periodic doses of cold water on our unbecoming ardour and proposals for expanding the limited range of exchanges. At the same time, they would assure us that the next step would come sooner than we might expect. It did. They surprised us, as they were to do on a number of occasions over the coming months.

At the end of March, after the Merhav visit, I had formally requested consideration of the possibility of a return visit to Israel, in the near future. They responded by counselling patience and preaching the gradualist Chinese doctrine of step by step. Two weeks later, Deputy Departmental Director Liu called me at home on a Saturday morning and with unconcealed satisfaction, informed me that it had been decided to accept our invitation for a return visit to Jerusalem, and that the Director of the Department would himself lead a small delegation.

Before we had time to digest these glad tidings, it was proposed that the visit take place from 22 April until 26 April. We were then at the end of the second week of April, with the week-long Passover festival pending, soon after which occurs Israel's Independence Day, with its official activities and ceremonies. This schedule was not favourable for the fixing of dates for so special a visit at such short notice. But within a day or two, we were able to agree to the dates proposed, allowing us about a week to prepare the visit.

This was the most encouraging development for which we could have hoped. Within less than two months of my arrival in Beijing, we would now be having an exchange of visits, for the first time, between the two countries' Foreign Ministries, at a very high level. It was also, of course, indicative. The March visit had not been rich in content, nor had it produced agreement on any new steps. It afforded us the opportunity to present our positions, lengthily and comprehensively, in places where they had not previously been heard, and detailed reports of these had been transmitted up and down the hierarchy. For their part, our hosts had publicly confirmed that there was no change in their Middle East policy, which they reiterated, and, in response to press leaks, had stated that there were no political contacts between China and Israel. Yet, despite the press leaks, including a Merhav interview with Kol Yisrael (Israel radio) on his visit, which they had specifically mentioned to us disapprovingly, it was now clear that they, too, had a programme for the development of exchanges on the official level, and a time-table in which gradualness and delay were not interminable. They continued to require that such exchanges remain entirely confidential, and that strict secrecy be maintained on both sides.

But first came Passover. My colleagues, together with two American Jewish young women engaged in business in Beijing, decided to organize an eve of Passover Seder, or festive meal ceremony, in which the story of the Exodus of the Jews from Egypt 3,500 years ago is recounted. It was held in the reception rooms of the apartment block in which we resided. About a hundred people came to this first ever Passover Seder in Beijing. Apart from a couple of score Jewish members of the foreign diplomatic corps and journalists, together with their families, we had several 'old timers' in Beijing, foreigners of Jewish origin and Communist conviction who had been living in China for decades, working for the government. Most had Chinese wives and, in some cases, Chinese grandchildren. Two had family members living in Israel. One of them commented, 'I have not attended a Jewish ceremony since my own bar mitzvah' (confirmation ceremony for 13 year-olds), and another, 'this is the first Passover Seder I have ever attended'.

These people were now in their seventies and eighties. They called to mind the punch-line of an old Jewish story, 'that is what must happen when you grow old – you become a Jew'. Dedicated, elderly Communists of western origin, they were not about to repent and revert to the customs of their forefathers, together with their Chinese offspring and descendants. But it was intriguing that they chose to come to a Jewish ceremonial gathering in Beijing, and that they felt, and *were* free to do so. Two years later, when we found it necessary to collect a payment for participation, to cover the expenses of what had become an annual gathering, a smaller number of such 'co-religionists' participated. Perhaps the novelty had worn off. But for us, this occasion was certainly another 'first' in Beijing. We were contacted by the Israeli media, and the gathering was reported in a number of foreign newspapers. Deputy Prime Minister and Foreign Minister, David Levy, telephoned to convey Passover greetings to the gathering. This, too, gave us the feeling of creating new beginnings.

A few days later, my luncheon guest was a prominent Chinese journalist, to whom I boasted of the first ever Passover Seder in Beijing, adding, for his particular benefit, that several of his Party and press friends and colleagues, foreign residents of Beijing of Jewish origin, had participated. His response was quite unexpected: 'Excuse me for saying this to you', he said, and after the slightest pause, 'to you as a Jew; but so many Jewish communists were strict ideologists, who made it more difficult for flexible, less oppressive views to prevail.' I was completely taken aback and offered no rebuttal. Whom was I to defend, or criticize under the circumstances? Even citing the example and courage of the Jewish dissidents ('refuseniks') in the USSR would have been irrelevant, and even tactless. However, the host government surely took note of the assemblage of foreign co-religionists and their families, the CNN, Reuters and UPI bureau chiefs and other journalists stationed in Beijing, and quite a number of foreign diplomats, particularly half a dozen families from the US Embassy. The myth of Jewish worldwide influence, particularly in the press, had certainly reached China, where it was coupled with profound respect, even reverence for the Jewish people, its ancient culture and contribution to civilization and human achievement. Our Chinese hosts constantly, almost routinely, welcomed Israeli visitors with their recital, these being China's highest historical values and its own unsurpassed mark of distinction in the annals of mankind. The impact of the myth and the semblance of power and influence it bestowed could only be helpful to us in the task in hand.

This was certainly true of the Chinese picture of Israel's standing and support in the United States. Chinese visitors to the US found themselves constantly encountering Jews and friends of Israel. For reasons unclear, except in obvious cases in which US hosts queried their Chinese guests about relations with Israel (at our prompting or otherwise), the Chinese were generally aware of 'Who is a Jew' in their US encounters. Relations between China and the US were, at best, dicey, with constant public and Congressional criticism of China on a variety of issues, from human rights to arms sales, coupled with the annual hue and cry in Washington DC and threats to discontinue Most Favoured Nation terms of trade with China. We did not seek official US help or guidance in pursuing our own contacts with China, their capacity to help being clearly very limited. Unlike nearly 40 years earlier, when the US had actively opposed the development of relations with China, they were now certainly not antagonistic to such efforts, even if unable to help. We were always made to feel very welcome in the US Embassy, and they generously provided guidance, whenever sought. The impression in Beijing that so many 'overseas Jews', to borrow a term from 'overseas Chinese', were active and prominent in US public life, was a highly positive factor in Chinese views and assessments of Israel.

The three-man delegation to Israel from the West Asian and North African Department was to include the Department Director and the Deputy Director of the Division covering Israel and its neighbours. We were informed in advance that they would be bringing 'some new proposals in the bilateral area'. This was mentioned prior to the items of regional matters and the Middle East peace process, as presented to us in preparatory discussions in Beijing on the agenda. They repeated their requirement that the visit be kept secret. While assuring them that we would do all we could in that respect, we sought to explain the ubiquitous nature of the press in Israel and the eye-catching rarity of Chinese visitors. Their response, delivered with impassive expression, was that they relied on us.

At this period, the Israeli Foreign Ministry had one department in charge of relations with Africa, Asia and Australasia. On the Asian continental land mass (excluding Tokyo, Manila and Singapore), there were only three Israeli Embassies. It was a department not unaccustomed to secret visits and exchanges, involving some of the numerous states of Africa and Asia with which there were no diplomatic relations. Yet, for the departmental personnel involved in this first visit from China, it was a very special experience in their professional careers. For Israel's foreign relations, and certainly for those entrusted with day-to-day contacts with Asia, diplomatic relations with China were surely the great and glittering prize. Everything possible was done to ensure minimal exposure at Ben-Gurion Airport. The delegation was driven from the tarmac to a special VIP room, and from there, guests and hosts left for Jerusalem. The five lengthy working sessions, extending over three days, were held in the hotel where the guests were lodged. This avoided unnecessary exposure in the Foreign Ministry corridors, and at its entrance and exit, where journalists move about freely, unlike the Foreign Ministry in Beijing. Only the meeting with Deputy Prime Minister Levy was held in his office, in the ministerial compound.

At the first session, the Chinese side expressed their appreciation of the privilege of being the first representatives of the Chinese government to visit Israel officially. They went further, adding that they were not satisfied with the level of contacts and the secrecy of the visit. They looked forward to open visits and at a higher level (presumably referring to the political level), but at this point such developments were contingent, they added, upon progress in the Middle East peace process. Addressing themselves to the agenda for the discussions, they raised the proposals which they had brought with them, as mentioned in our prior exchanges in Beijing concerning the agenda. After that, they gave us their responses to specific proposals and requests raised by Director General Merhav during his visit the previous month.

On the first point, they noted with satisfaction that the political and other contacts and exchanges between the two countries were now being conducted on an ongoing basis in the two capitals, no longer in Hong Kong or New York. For its part, China would seek to promote and extend these contacts. They expressed optimism in that respect, subject to the general Middle East situation – a proviso which was invariably appended at this period. They presented their proposals for extending to the two representative offices, in Beijing and Tel Aviv, privileges and authority which were calculated to facilitate the expansion of activities and exchanges. These would include additional consular authority, the availability of customary diplomatic communication facilities (between representative office and home base), as well as privileges, immunities and exemptions as provided under the 1961 Vienna Convention. This would mean a considerable extension of facilities but no change of formal status. The offices would continue to represent the China International Tourist Service (CITS) on the one hand, and the Israel Academy of Sciences and Humanities. There would be no official emblems or flags, nor diplomatic licence plates or identification. But diplomatic passports would now be mutually recognized and used by the senior personnel of the two offices, while staff members would continue to use official service passports. Appropriate official identity cards would be issued by the respective authorities, indicating privileges and immunities.

These proposals constituted a considerable step forward towards the goal of official relations and status, as opposed to the hitherto explicitly non-governmental profile and functions of the two offices. The Israeli side was very pleased with this Chinese initiative. It would afford us the privileges and status enjoyed by the Israeli representatives in Moscow, as our Chinese guests commented outside the framework of the working sessions. Our colleagues in Moscow were under the jurisdiction of the Netherlands Embassy, as part of the Israel Interests Section of that Embassy, which had taken care of Israel's interests in the USSR since the rupture of diplomatic relations between the two countries in 1967, in the aftermath of the Six Day War. They were now permitted to use the former Israeli Embassy building, as an annex of the Netherlands Embassy, to house its Israel Interests Section. Even though the comparison was formally inaccurate, it was significant that our guests should raise it. They were clearly making comparisons with our status in Moscow and being wary of not going further than the Soviets. This was not the only occasion on which the Chinese would evoke this comparison in discussions on the formal status of our relations and contacts.

Their responses to the points raised by Merhav in Beijing were also largely positive and encouraging. The previous year, following agreement between the two Foreign Ministers on an exchange of students at their annual encounter at the UN General Assembly, five Israeli Chinese-language students had arrived in Szechuan, and five Chinese students had been placed in Hebrew classes at the Hebrew University in Jerusalem. The Israeli students were almost as far away from our office in Beijing as they were from home. We had asked that the next group, due to arrive at the end of the summer of 1991, be located closer to Beijing, and in a Mandarin-speaking area. The Szechuan dialect is very different from Mandarin. Our guests now informed us that they were, indeed, seeking to locate a campus which would meet these two requirements.

There were similarly positive responses on specific proposals for cultural exchanges, which were to lead to the first-ever appearance of a Chinese performing group (acrobats) in Israel later in the year. They also confirmed the pending visit to Israel, as guests of the Israel Academy of Sciences and Humanities, of a delegation of the Chinese Academy of Sciences, the host organization of our Beijing Liaison Office. The delegation would be led by the Academy's Vice-President, a distinguished and prestigious scientist, and an agreement to be concluded on regular exchanges between the two academies would give a boost to bilateral, scientific and tech-nological exchanges. In the medical and banking fields, too, contacts and exchanges were agreed upon.

Only in the area of direct trade between the two countries and of contacts with the responsible Ministry in Beijing did there appear to be no progress. Our assessment of the situation in this regard was that the powerful Ministry of Foreign Economic Relations and Trade, as it was then called, continued to be concerned with possible fall-out and negative implications for China's trade relations with the Arab world. Later in the year, we found a way to make contacts with this Ministry, by a circuitous route, with one of its subordinate agencies. Subsequently, with the visit of a delegation from the Israeli Chamber of Commerce, we made our first direct contacts with the Ministry's officials.

The Israeli side briefed its guests at length on the ongoing contacts with the US, Soviets and Egyptians concerning the peace process, on our assessments of the Middle East situation in general and Arab regimes in particular, and of future developments in the area. At their request, we presented a review of the state of our relations with the USSR and the Eastern European countries. On the central issue of how to promote a Middle East peace process, they posed two questions, indicative of their own thinking. Why did Israel oppose UN participation in the proposed regional conference, and Palestine Liberation Organisation participation or any direct contacts and negotiations with the PLO? The Chinese position gave preference to direct negotiations between the parties to a dispute, and China had always viewed the PLO as the sole legitimate representative of the Palestinian people. China had recognized the state of Palestine, as proclaimed by Chairman Arafat in 1988, and the PLO representative in Beijing had assumed the full status of Ambassador. Failing direct negotiations, the Chinese viewed as natural inter-mediary the recognised international body in which China occupied its proper place, i.e. the UN and its Security Council. They appeared to indicate that China's support for any other avenue of negotiation acceptable to the parties to the dispute came in third place, after direct negotiations or UN mediation.

A special working session was devoted to a detailed presentation of China's Middle East policies. Fundamental to their positions was the view that the Palestine question and the Israeli–Arab dispute are at the heart of the Middle East problem and the main cause of regional instability. In a nice gesture of balance, this point was followed by expressions of appreciation for Israel's restraint during the Gulf War, when Iraqi Scud missiles fell on Israel but Israel did not retaliate against Iraq, thereby avoiding further complication of the hostilities. It had become standard Chinese practice to express, in our dialogues, approval of this Israeli restraint. Had Israel reacted, as might certainly have been expected, her military involvement against Iraq, however manifestly justified as self-defence against unilateral Iraqi aggression, would have added enormous difficulties to the already complex US task of keeping the Gulf War alliance together, particularly its Arab support. It might have been thought that this aspect of the problem would be less disturbing to China, unhappy as she was with the further display of US 'hegemonism', in creating and leading the Gulf War alliance. But China's real concern arose from her basic interest in peaceful solutions to inter-national disputes, with minimum damage to the countries and regions involved and their economic and trading potential. Israeli intervention or reaction to Iraqi aggression against her would certainly have added to the sum total of physical and economic damage, as well as further complicating the hostilities between Israel and her neighbours, which China viewed as the 'heart', or 'core', of the Middle East dispute and regional instability.

The Chinese side proceeded to spell out six basic elements or principles essential, in China's view, in the search for a commonly agreed solution. Restoration of the territories, in accordance with UN resolutions, and taking into account Israel's security, was the key to any solution. The problem of reconciling withdrawal and security for Israel could be viewed as a classic Chinese 'contradiction' (*maodun*). Like other advocates of withdrawal, the Chinese offered the formula of Israel's security being best served and assured by peace with her neighbours, itself conditional upon withdrawal. Such a withdrawal, they asserted, was the surest and most effective means of achieving security and peace. The opposite view, that it could be the surest and most effective means of initiating renewed aggression against Israel and laying the groundwork for a threat to Israel's very existence was, at the very least, equally arguable and remained unanswered.

The second element concerned the role of the UN in the peace process. The Chinese position was that peace negotiations should take place in the framework of an international conference, convened under UN auspices and with the participation of the five permanent members of the Security Council, as well as all the parties (including the PLO) involved in the dispute. This framework assured a role for China, as a permanent member of the Council. This also happened to be a basic element in Arab and PLO requirements for a process of negotiation. Israel was opposed to a major UN role, because of the powerful voice of the many hostile Arab and Moslem member states in UN deliberations, supported and, at times, instigated and led in anti-Israel initiatives and proposals by the Communist bloc. As the months were to progress towards the convening of the Madrid Conference, at the end of October 1991, less would be heard from the Chinese, both in their public statements and in their dialogue with us, about their advocacy of UN auspices and more and more of their support for any other process acceptable to the parties. This was consistent with the pragmatism in Chinese policy, and their interest in solutions to problems rather than dogmatic positions or formulas.

This latter pragmatic position was already indicated in the third element enumerated, the desirability of bilateral and multilateral dialogue, inferring support for Israel's efforts to negotiate or conduct secret talks with Arab parties, either directly or through third party mediation, and particularly the joint US–Soviet efforts to convene a meeting of the parties. They added that such contacts were not antithetical to the international conference concept but, in fact, complementary.

The Chinese side reiterated its advocacy of comprehensive and balanced disarmament. All types of weapons, conventional and otherwise, should be included, in order to achieve real disarmament, and in the process care must be taken to avoid any temporary, dangerous imbalances being created. Support was expressed for regional arrangements amongst the states concerned, involving co-operation and mutual inspection and assurances. It was again stated that China plays a minor role in arms exports to the region. China advocates responsibility in the supply of arms. Its sales of arms contribute solely to defensive capability and requirements, without affecting regional military balances or threatening stability; nor do they constitute or create intervention in the internal affairs of the purchasing state.

China's Five Principles of Peace and Coexistence were presented as a fifth, essential element in creating new relations and a peaceful order in the Middle East. Peace between Israel and her neighbours can only be maintained if founded upon a basis of justice and equality. The Five Principles, first enunciated in a Sino-Indian agreement concluded by Premiers Zhou and Nehru in 1954, were again embraced by post-Cultural Revolution China and incorporated into the 1982 Party Constitution. They are mutual respect for territorial integrity and sovereignty; non-aggression; non-interference in internal affairs; equality and mutual benefit; peaceful co-existence.

Finally, confidence-building measures and behaviour are required from all parties, to create an atmosphere conducive to dialogue and negotiations. As a Security Council permanent member, China is committed to peaceful solutions of international problems.

It advocates responsible policies to that end, creating mutual trust. In this connection, the Chinese Head of Delegation commented that the negotiation process would be prolonged and arduous, and that much patience and commitment would be required for the achievement of agreement. This was a very Chinese comment, reflecting not only the national characteristic of patience, but also the wisdom of experience and understanding of the complexity of problems. Haste is not Chinese, but rather awareness of complexities and subtleties, combined with a traditional view of time and its expanses. This was to be demonstrated time and again, by their tolerant patience throughout the ups and downs of the Middle East peace negotiations over the ensuing couple of years. They appeared to have not only more patience but more faith in the negotiation process than its actual participants, and future exchanges in the Beijing Foreign Ministry parlours at difficult and critical junctures in the peace process could well be described as soothing. Their only consistent urging was for flexibility, from all sides and parties to the negotiations.

China had its own views on the essential contents of a solution. These were spelled out from time to time in the UN and elsewhere, or summarized in Premier Li's Five Points. Our guests took the opportunity of presenting them in detail. China supports the national rights of the Palestinian people. The PLO is its internationally recognized representative and should fulfil this role in the peace process and negotiations. The PLO had accepted and recognized the reality of the existence of Israel in 1988, in China's view, and had thereby abandoned earlier aspirations to drive the Jews into the sea. In the past, the late Premier Zhou Enlai had himself rejected and urged his Arab interlocutors to abandon such aspirations. Israel should have direct contacts with the PLO, as the Chinese Communist Party had recently decided to have with the Kuomintang Party in Taiwan. Both sides must seek to free themselves from the past and move forward to a future of peace. China senses a change, to a variation of more pragmatic attitudes on the part of the Arab States towards Israel.

There was no 'hard sell' in the above presentation. Apart from being a statement of Chinese policy, it was clearly an effort to contribute to 'liberating minds' – ours – from the old patterns and ideas, and opening them up to fresh thinking. This Dengist slogan, aimed at facilitating the 'four modernizations' and the 'opening up to the outside world' policy, employed the terminology of the 1949 liberation to urge the need for a new form of revolutionary liberation, of the mind. A comparison of these positions with Chinese press comment at the time indicates how far official China, or at least foreign policy cadres and decision-makers, were moving towards a more balanced standpoint. The press would tend to lag behind changes in nuance. It takes time for the media in China to grasp incipient changes, and the tendency is to play safe and continue to present the familiar line and language, pending explicit instructions.

The *Beijing Review* of 1-7/4/1991 (Shi Jian, 'Possible Solution to Middle East Question', p. 4) presented China's traditional view of the core of the Middle East problem as being the Palestine question, 'with its crux being Israel's invasion and expansion against Palestine and other Arab countries'. Amongst the points for a solution listed in the article was the stipulation that 'Israel must stop its suppression of the Palestine people'. An editorial in the *People's Daily* of 8/4/1991 harshly criticized 'Israel's stubborn positions', and her alleged refusal to negotiate or to recognise the PLO. Other press comments during the month suggested only a continuity in China's positions. But the contents of our direct dialogue did indicate that changes were taking place, even if these were not yet reflected in the official press or even communicated to all the branches of party and government. We were witnessing a process of change in policy towards Israel and the nature of contacts with us, as well as in formulations of policy on the Arab–Israeli dispute. At the same time, it appeared that such change within the monolithic and centralist Chinese system could also be a gradual process, without total agreement, coordination and identity of formulation necessarily accompanying every stage of the process and internal debate. It certainly appeared to us, at this stage, that the Ministry of Foreign Affairs was playing a 'leading role', to use an appropriate Party expression, while other official institutions continued to give expression to the old formulations and attitudes, in whatever pertained to Israel and contacts with us. But that, too, was soon to show signs of change.

The visitors were taken to visit a kibbutz, where they were given a comprehensive audio-visual presentation on its organization and development. While lawns and shrubbery were much appreciated, and interest was expressed in the workshops and kibbutz industry, as well as in the agriculture, there was something less than enthusiasm for the idea of kibbutz society. The Chinese pass their lives within the family and extended family unit, and on a peasant farm. Even if the commune system, which had been imposed upon much of China's land and peasantry, had proved an economic success, it would have remained alien to the generation on which it was imposed. The most effective and successful economic measure of the post-Cultural Revolution and post-Mao regime was the abolition of a great part of the agricultural commune system and the restoration of family farming on commune land, leased out under a 'contract responsibility system', bringing with it the renewal of the family unit, home and kitchen. During the Cultural Revolution, the commune system had extended even to the kitchen, introducing into the countryside the aberration of communal dining.

It was not to be expected that Chinese guests would be impressed with the kibbutz. Perhaps their kibbutz hosts could have elicited more enthusiasm, had they stressed the voluntarism and idealism of the system. But these belonged to a bygone age, even in Israel. Questions raised related to the economy of the kibbutz, and varying attitudes to work amongst the members. The economy of the kibbutz movements and the viability of very many kibbutzim have been severely challenged for some years in Israel. As a social experiment, it could hardly commend itself to the Chinese, in view of their own experience. Its special role in the development of Jewish farming and land settlement in Israel belonged to a past, with which only a limited number of visitors to Israel are concerned; amongst these, the contemporary Chinese are pragmatic seekers of solutions to the problems and challenges of today and tomorrow, forever pushing ahead and preferring trial and error to historical examinations and conclusions. This may not appear very Marxist. A Chinese story of the mid-1970s, when Mao was reported in the *People's Daily* as belittling Deng's knowledge of Marxist-Leninism, had the Dengists responding that *his* forte was 'market-Leninism'.

The visit had been a milestone in the development of official relations between China and Israel. The very fact that it had taken place, the length and depth of the dozen or more hours of discussions and working sessions, of becoming familiar with each other's positions and thinking, and the fact that these would be fully reported up and down the echelons of government and Party in Beijing, with the thoroughness and efficiency which characterize official reporting and communication within the Chinese bureaucracy, had the effect of a major step forward towards mutual acceptance, familiarity and recognition. The Chinese proposals for extending the privileges and authority of the two representative offices were a significant practical expression and indication of such a step forward. Some of our people attributed the proposals to inconveniences and difficulties experienced by the Tel Aviv CITS office, viewing them as designed to make life and work easier for the CITS representatives in Israel. This was a very restricted reading of the situation. In the context of the developing contacts between the two countries, these proposals were intended by the Chinese to promote and expand relations and exchanges. The various stages of Chinese contacts and exchanges of offices with the United States and Singapore in the past, and with South Korea in the period immediately preceding the 1992 establishment of diplomatic relations, were of a similar nature and followed comparable paths.

Our assessment of the next stage was that further development in formal relations would now be contingent upon progress in the Middle East peace process. This had been stated in so many words by our guests. On the other hand, we were now in a better position to develop informal relations and mutual exchanges on the 'people to people' level, of non-governmental and unofficial visitors and delegations, as well as of confidential official exchanges, within limits to be explored.

Inevitably, there were reports in the Israeli press on the visit, the composition of the Chinese delegation, their meeting with Deputy Prime Minister and Foreign Minister Levy, and even the hotel where they stayed was identified. This displeased the guests; but the question for us was whether they were becoming accustomed to Israeli indiscretion and press leaks, or would they be more wary and reserved in future contacts. Perhaps the answer to that depended less on the Israeli press reports and more on Arab reactions to those reports of the visit, particularly on the vehemence of Arab protests and those of their friends in Beijing.

5
Digging in

DURING THE week of the talks with the Chinese delegation in Jerusalem, a small Knesset (Israel's parliament) delegation had arrived in Beijing, on its way to an Inter-Parliamentary Union meeting, to be held in North Korea. This was the first visit of an Israeli parliamentary group to China. There had been two or three individual visits of left-wing and Communist Party Knesset members in previous years, as guests of the Chinese Association for International Understanding, a friendship group associated with the International Liaison Department of the Communist Party Central Committee, but not an official organ of the party. We were now seeking to develop a normal routine of Israeli officials and delegations openly visiting or passing through Beijing.

They had received their visas from the CITS office in Tel Aviv. The visas carried the stamp of China's Hong Kong Consular authorities, just as visas issued by our Beijing office bore the stamp of our Hong Kong Consulate General. Not being official missions, we were not authorized to transact official business, at least not under our own imprimatur.

Before my departure for Israel, we had arranged a reception in honour of the visiting Knesset delegation, to be held in my Beijing apartment, and invitations had been sent out to our friends and contacts, including personnel of the West Asian and North African Department. The reception was held in my absence, hosted on my behalf by the Liaison Office Director, Dr Joseph Shalhevet and his wife. But the time was not yet ripe for Chinese Foreign Ministry personnel to participate in a reception given by us. Two officials of the staff of the National People's Congress (NPC) did attend, but no actual members of the Congress. These were our first contacts with NPC staff members, and they were to prove useful in the future.

Before leaving Jerusalem, I had instructed our Beijing office to invite the members of the Chinese delegation, on their return from their visit to Israel, to a dinner at my apartment on 30 April. I could not delay it, because we had the Israeli State Controller arriving that weekend, to participate in an international congress, and my Israeli Foreign Ministry colleague at our Beijing office, Yoel Guilatt, was due to leave for Israel early the following week. My secretary contacted the Foreign Ministry, and the initial response was surprisingly frank. They did not yet feel that it was appropriate for them to appear with us in a public place, such as a restaurant. Perhaps the frankness, rather than a polite refusal and excuses, arose from their wish to give us the option of 'privatizing' the invitation in an acceptable manner, or to clarify the bounds and limitations of our contacts. In either case, I had my secretary reply that the invitation was not to a public place or restaurant but to my apartment. The reaction to this was a query concerning other invitees, indicating that they could not openly attend a dinner at my home, in the presence of others, just as their colleagues had not attended the reception in honour of the Knesset members. I instructed my secretary to convey that the only other participants would be our own staff members. At that point, the invitations were accepted.

The dinner was a happy first occasion for us to meet socially, rather than formally, with our Departmental colleagues from the Chinese Foreign Ministry. The atmosphere was warm, almost intimate, after the four days spent together with three of their number in Israel, the previous week. I did not yet even have a dinner-table to seat the 10 guests. It was still being put together in a local carpentry shop. We managed to hire a table from a nearby hotel and bring it into the apartment that day.

At dinner, our guests were effusive in their expressions of appreciation for the hospitality of the previous week and were obviously as pleased to be having dinner with us in Beijing for the first time, as we were ourselves. From the dinner-table talk, it emerged that of their own initiative, they had seen more than we knew of Jerusalem. We had, one morning, strolled with them down past the Montefiore

Windmill, facing Mount Zion, and had suggested crossing the valley, up to the Jaffa Gate and the Citadel. They had demurred, in deference to what they understood to be Arab objections to foreign guests visiting the Old City in the company of Israeli official hosts. Apparently, they had later taken a cab to the Old City. They were surprised, incredulous that we were unaware of it, indicating more respect than was warranted for our supervision and channels of information.

During the evening, our guests raised the idea, as if spontaneously, of inviting my colleagues and myself to luncheon, as their guests. This was intended as an expression of appreciation for our hospitality during their visit to Israel, and as a farewell to Guilatt. The following day was a public holiday. We were back at our desks the morning after, when a call came from the West Asian and North African Department inviting my two colleagues and myself to luncheon that day. The venue was the Beijing Roast Duck restaurant, a much frequented landmark in the heart of the city and a commercial enterprise owned by the municipal government.

What had happened, from one day to the next, to make it now possible for us to appear together in so public a place? We could only speculate or conclude that the Department had authority and leeway in determining and managing the extent and openness of their contacts with us, in such a way as to avoid unnecessary friction with Arab States, relations with which were, of course, in its area of responsibility. In this case, the exigencies of keeping their public distance from us may simply have been moderated by Chinese conviviality and warmth, with their ingrained sense of hospitality taking priority over counsels of gradualness. This small step forward certainly came sooner than expected, to recall our hosts' assurance on an earlier occasion.

We were, indeed, espied in the company of the Foreign Ministry official designated to receive us on the steps leading into the restaurant lobby, by a number of friends, including two foreign diplomats. They subsequently telephoned to enquire how far the silken curtain of secrecy had been raised.

I had been in Beijing less than two months, and the progress was surely encouraging. Not only did we have a good working relationship and personal rapport with the Department, but our two

Ministries were no longer strangers to each other. Previously, the Ministers themselves had met in New York annually since 1987. Now, we had together established a range of normal contacts, from the level of Vice Minister and Director General down to Department and Division levels. In the next few days, Israel's flag was to be hoisted in Beijing for the first time, together with those of the other countries of the delegates to the Asian meeting of State Controllers and Auditors.

In these early weeks in China, not only had the contacts between the two Foreign Ministries undergone profound change, but so had Beijing. The cold, damp and darkened skies of late winter, camouflaged by mists of coal-smoke from a million heating ducts and chimneys, had given way to long, bright sunny days and blue skies, revealing the mountains girding the city to the north and west. Trees and shrubs were budding and sprouting along every road and highway, and spring flowers abounded. The dark, dull clothing of winter had given way to coats of many colours, and to attractively attired young ladies. Spring is festive in Beijing, as elsewhere. For the stranger and visitor, each corner reveals its own fresh beauty and previously hidden charms. Colours, activity in the streets, stores and markets, the very faces of the people and their smiles all seem to take on a special, joyous air at this time of the year. The Chinese can be sharp critics, with their lively intellects, but they balance this with memory of a past of suffering, shortages and famine, without dwelling on them. Critical as they can be of the present, every day is a festive day of plenty and well-being, as compared with the harsh rigours of the Great Leap Forward and the ensuing famine, in which more than twenty million people died from starvation, and the Cultural Revolution. But in China, memory can go back very much further, to past centuries and millennia of rural poverty, virtual serfdom, and the periods of chaos when collapse of central authority exposed the masses of the peasantry to extreme hardship and deprivation. Without dwelling on the past, the Chinese people know how to count their blessings. They are essentially forward looking, even as they let loose barbs of criticism at bureaucracy, government, economic management or the cost of heating fuel.

Every day of spring is like a festival, especially Sundays, when all Beijing, families, young couples, oldsters, youth groups, bicycles and cycle-powered rickshaws throng the streets. Bright and early, relaxed and happy families swarm through the parks, with the single child, dressed up to the hilt, at the centre of the attentive ensemble of parents and grandparents. Ribbons and flags, street bands and propaganda booths add to the *perpetuum mobile* and bustling activity. The booths and street tables on one Sunday in May 1991, were doling out literature and good counsel on family planning, side by side with the 'explain to the people the importance of taxation' campaign and its banners. The markets and shops are in full swing. At the ubiquitous building sites, even on the day of rest, the contract labourers from the countryside surge over walls, pits, wire-frames and skeletal edifices. They often work at night, by searchlight, particularly in seasons of favourable weather, so that they can take several days off to visit their distant homes.

At this time, I was privileged to be invited for the first time into a Chinese home. In Beijing, the vast majority now live in huge apartment blocks. Unlike the old courtyard dwellings (*hutongs*), where a number of families – no longer a single or extended family – live each in one of the small one-storey structures surrounding the communal yard, the apartment blocks have running water, toilets, showers and basic modern conveniences. Housing is provided by the work unit and is part of the 'iron rice bowl' system, guaranteeing employees life tenure, wages and pensions, and a variety of social and welfare services. Monthly rents are about $2–$3 per month, less than 5 per cent of an average salary.

The stairwells are not maintained or cleaned and appear never to have been repainted. Bicycles are piled up at the entrances. Front doors to the apartments are like shapeless slabs of wood. The apartments are furnished simply, by western standards. Concrete or stone floors may or may not be partially covered with linoleum, or a small rug, and windows are often without curtains. The kitchen is merely an extension or corner of the living room, partitioned off with a large piece of furniture or curtain. There will be a television set, usually coloured, and a small refrigerator. Some families have washing machines.

The Chinese are familiar with living standards elsewhere, from television and foreign movies. They are not accustomed to inviting foreigners into their homes, and this is not only a result of past supervision and control of contacts with foreigners, and of the wary eye of the block janitor. They are a proud and sensitive people, and they will not embarrass themselves or their visitors by exposing them to comparisons of housing and living standards. In an entirely impersonal situation, however, Chinese hospitality towards strangers asserts itself. On more than one occasion, escorting foreign visitors in lanes and alleys, and poking one's nose into the old court-yards, some of which are still very picturesque, my visitors and I were invited into a courtyard home, usually barely more than one or one and a half rooms, and offered tea.

However simple the apartment and furnishings, the hospitality and food are incomparable. Quite apart from the expense involved in offering alcohol, choice fruits and confectionery, home-cooking in China is very important indeed, and the variety of dishes offered is to be described as a banquet, matched only by the graciousness and warmth of the Chinese hosts. Official entertainment is regular practice in China. On a business visit, the foreigner will find himself being hosted or playing host at dinner each evening, and often at luncheon. All such entertaining takes place in restaurants. Rarely did any of the hundreds of such meals in restaurants over the years, however fine many of them were, compare in the culinary sense with the food served on the few occasions on which I was invited to private homes.

In the mid-1980s, China started issuing entry visas on Israeli passports to official participants in international meetings and conventions held in China. During previous decades, only on very rare occasions were Israeli passports recognized and accepted by visa issuing authorities. No instance is known before the 1955 Hacohen delegation visit, as guests of the Chinese Foreign Ministry. From then until the Cultural Revolution, there are two or three recorded instances, in which visas were issued to an Israeli par-ticipant in an international youth delegation and to an Israeli Ambassador to Moscow and his wife, for a private visit. Not until the early 1980s, when China was embarked upon her policy of opening to the outside world and again began to host international gatherings, were there instances of Israeli scientists and other specialists receiving Chinese visas on their passports. In many of these cases, it was only after repeated requests made to the Chinese hosts or official authorities by the sponsoring international body that a visa, initially refused, would subsequently be granted, in a foreign capital, often too late for the passport holder to travel on to China in time for the conference, from whichever city and Chinese Consulate he had been awaiting the tardy authorization from Beijing.

Not only was there no arrangement for receiving a visa in Israel, its availability or authorization could not be confirmed through tourist agency contacts. Even Israeli scholars working or residing abroad and joining a foreign group or delegation of their country of residence to an international conference held in China were singled out from the rest of the group and usually denied visas. Until the late 1980s, there was no such thing as Israeli tourism to China. Israeli tourists reaching China had been holders of other foreign passports. In the late 1980s, it became a little easier for Israeli delegates to conferences in China and even for an occasional Israeli tourist group to receive visas, as was the case with a youth delegation to a conference hosted by the Beijing municipality in spring, 1990. By this time, CITS had its office in Tel Aviv but was not yet authorized to issue visas, and an Israeli official had been in Beijing for some months, preparing the opening of the Beijing Liaison Office (officially opened in June, 1990). In fact, Israeli visitors sponsored by the CITS office, or by a Chinese host organisation, had to receive their visas elsewhere, as in my own case, as late as March 1991. Even at this period, several requests for intervention, directly from the Liaison Office to the Foreign Ministry in Beijing, were often required, before visas were authorized and issued.

The first visas issued by the CITS office in Tel Aviv were to the members of the Knesset delegation, to travel via Beijing to the Inter-Parliamentary Union meeting in Pyongyang, as earlier mentioned. The visit of the Israeli State Controller, leading a small delegation from her office to participate in a conference of her Asian colleagues in Beijing early in May, was the first occasion of an official delegation, led by a senior Israeli government functionary, and consisting of government employees, being openly received in Beijing, as guests of a Chinese official, governmental host body, in this case the Auditing Administration of the State Council. This delegation, too, had been issued with visas by the Tel Aviv CITS office.

When the national flags of the participating delegations in this Asian conference were flown over the building in which it was held, Israel's flag made its first public appearance, and some of our friends paid special visits to the building, to see Israel's flag flying aloft in China's capital on this first occasion. On a previous occasion, a request to hoist the Israeli flag, together with those of other national delegations to a conference in Beijing, resulted in all the flags being taken down. The formal reason given was that in the absence of diplomatic relations, China's practice and protocol did not permit the use of national flags and symbols. We had no doubt that this was due to China's being wary about displaying contacts with Israel and inviting opposition or protest, whether from its Arab friends or Moslem Chinese groups. Eight months were to elapse before the Israeli flag would again be publicly raised in Beijing's streets, for the visit of Deputy Prime Minister and Foreign Minister Levy and the conclusion of the agreement on diplomatic relations.

A Deputy Auditor General and a Judge of the Supreme Court attended a luncheon, arranged by our office but formally offered by the Israeli State Controller, in honour of her conference hosts. This was the first occasion on which there was participation at the Chinese government level in an event hosted by an Israeli official visitor. During the conference proceedings, the Israeli State Controller and her two colleagues were accorded all the appropriate attentions, including platform appearances. The Controller was received by a Vice President of the Supreme Court. It had taken us two weeks to arrange this, during which time the host authorities were presumably weighing up the question of whether to make this extra official gesture, the Israeli Controller being herself a former Supreme Court Judge.

This level of treatment of the Israeli visitor arose naturally from the circumstances of official Israeli participation in an international meeting hosted by a Chinese government agency. The participation was itself a development in relations. Previous international meetings in Beijing, attended by Israeli academics and professionals, had been hosted by various academic and specialized institutions. Extending previous practice and creating new relationships and precedents was precisely what we were now there to do and directly promoted our goal of normalization of official contacts.

With the Ministry of Foreign Affairs, we held ongoing discussions during the late spring on a 'non-paper' defining the proposed new privileges and status of the two offices. In the course of these discussions, a West Asian and North African Department desk officer paid a first official visit to our offices (in an official vehicle), in order to clarify one or two details of the non-paper. I had been at the Ministry the previous day and again that morning, and in the absence of Guilatt (in Israel), whom they would routinely have invited to deal with these details, they sent their man to me. This was very courteous. We were pleased to be given this further evidence of the Chinese wish to expedite agreement on the new status and privileges, and even more so to receive a first business visit from the Ministry to our Liaison Office.

The second of my two visits to the Ministry that week had also constituted a new 'step forward' in our contacts. For the first time, an appointment was arranged for me to meet with an officer from a Department other than West Asia and North Africa. I was received by an International Organizations Department officer, to discuss, at our request, a matter concerning one of the UN specialized agencies. This meant an extension of the bilateral political dialogue from its mainly mid-east dimension to the wider area of international organizations and their agenda.

Three Israeli journalists, representing the periodical press, came to Beijing during May, as guests of the Chinese periodical press group. They were the first Israeli journalists to be granted visas to come to China. This was complementary to the half dozen visits to Israel of Chinese journalists, initiated or encouraged by our Jerusalem Department or ourselves, during the previous 18 months. At the Beijing dinner given in their honour by the New China News Agency (Xinhua), with the participation of a couple of dozen local journalists, mainly from the periodicals, I was again addressed as Excellency and Mr Ambassador, coupled with toasts expressing the hope for diplomatic relations. The journalists must have been issued with some instructions concerning contacts with our office and its status, but they certainly appeared to have lots of leeway, even to the point of expressing unconcealed support – but not in print – for diplomatic relations between the two countries, and in addressing me as a diplomat.

1. Reuven Merhav on the Great Wall in March 1991 with Ruth Kahanov, the author's assistant in Beijing

2. The Israeli Foreign Ministry delegation on a secret visit (later acknowledged) touring an agricultural station north of Beijing

3. Deputy Prime Minister and Foreign Minister David Levy with his colleagues on the Great Wall during his first visit

4. The November 1991 meeting between Vice-Premier Wu Xueqian and Dani Gillerman, President of Israel's Chamber of Commerce

5. The signing on 24 January 1992, in the Diaoyutai, the official Guest House in Beijing

6. Toasting official relations

中国日报

CHINA DAILY

China's
'English-language Newspaper
Edited and
Published in Beijing
also
Printed in Shanghai, Guangzhou, Xi'an
Hong Kong and New York

Vol. 11 No. 3272   Saturday, January 25, 1992   Price: 30 fen; 35 fen (airmail)

China and Israel start diplomatic relations

by our staff reporter
Zhang Ping

China and Israel established full diplomatic relations yesterday in Beijing, opening a new era for co-operation between China and the Jewish state.

Visiting Israeli Foreign Minister David Levy and his Chinese counterpart Qian Qichen signed the agreement at Beijing's Diaoyutai State Guesthouse setting up ties on the ambassadorial level.

The two sides said that the establishment of Israel ties between China and Israel would push forward the on-going Middle East peace process.

"China will make efforts to help push forward the peace talks," Qian told reporters.

He noted that China has good relations with Arab countries and can make help out in this regard.

Chinese Vice Foreign Minister Yang Fuchang is scheduled to take part in the next round of Middle East peace talks due to take place in Moscow on Tuesday.

He will be the first Chinese representative to participate in the

flexible attitude so as to enable the talks to make progress in accordance with the relevant United Nations resolutions.

He said that China expresses its deep sympathy with the Jewish nation's sufferings in history.

During the meeting, Levy briefed the Chinese Premier on Israel's views on the Middle East situation, saying that the Middle East peace process has brought hope to the people.

During the talks between Chinese and Israeli foreign ministers, both of them vowed to strengthen bilateral co-operation and make concerted efforts to promote peace in the world.

Levy gave an account of Israeli developments in various fields, including agriculture, science and technology, culture and trade, saying that the two countries can co-operate in these fields.

Qian said the two countries can make contacts in these fields, exchanging information and gradually conduct co-operation.

Now that the Middle East peace talks are under way, China wel-

Chinese State Councillor and Foreign Minister Qian Qichen (right) and visiting Israeli Deputy Prime Minister and Foreign Minister David Levy shake hands after signing a joint communique on the establishment of diplomatic relations between China and Israel at the Diaoyutai State Guesthouse in Beijing yesterday.

China Daily photo by Wang Wenlan

Bank set to provide ¥6 billion for housing

by our staff reporter
Zhang Yu'an

The People's Construction Bank of China, a key financial source for country's fixed assets investment, yesterday announced a plan to provide at least 6 billion yuan ($1.15 billion) in loans this year to support the nationwide housing reform drive.

The figure represents a rise of 39 per cent from last year's 4.3 billion yuan ($813.3 million), and a substantial portion of this year's loans will be lent to individuals to enable them to purchase public housing offered for sale by the government, its president, Zhou Daojiong, said.

The State Council, China's highest governing body, has decided to accelerate housing reform in 1992, aiming to improve the living conditions of millions of urban residents, by building more housing for sale to individuals with funds raised through public, business and private channels.

Subsidies

Housing reform is also expected to reduce the country's financial burden caused by heavy subsidies on housing about 200 million fixed in cities and towns.

Zhou said that the bank, as the country's sole financial body specializing in fixed assets investment

7. The *China Daily*, 25 January 1992
8. The Foreign Minister of China, Qian Qichen, with his Israeli counterpart and the author

9. David Levy with the author after unveiling the plaque of the new embassy, 26 January 1992
10. The author presents his credentials to President Yang Shangkun

中 华 人 民 共 和 国 外 交 部

（92）部亚非字第107号

以色列国驻华大使馆：

　　中华人民共和国外交部向以色列国驻华大使馆致意，
并谨就大使馆一九九二年二月十一日来照答复如下：

　　中华人民共和国政府同意以色列国政府任命泽夫·苏
赋特先生为以色列国驻中华人民共和国特命全权大使。

　　顺致最崇高的敬意。

一九九二年　　月　　日于北京

No. 107 (92)
W.Asian & N.African Affairs Dept.

Embassy of Israel
Beijing, China

The Ministry of Foreign Affairs of the People´s Republic of
China presents its compliments to the Embassy of Israel in
Beijing and has the honour to reply in response to your note
dated February 11, 1992 as follows:

The Government of the People´s Republic of China expresses
agrément to the appointment of Mr. Zev Sufott by the
Government of the State of Israel as Ambassador Extraordinary
and Plenipotentiary of the State of Israel to the People´s
Republic of China.

The Ministry of Foreign Affairs of the People´s Republic of
China avails itself of this opportunity to renew to the
Embassy of Israel the assurances of its highest consideration.

Ministry of Foreign Affairs
People´s Republic of China
(Official Seal)
February 25, 1992, Beijing

11. China's confirmation of the author's appointment as ambassador,
25 February 1992

12. President Yang Shangkun and the author after the presentation

A visit to the Foreign Service College at this time illustrated some of the limitations and restraints. They received me hospitably but avoided taking me into the classrooms and exposing their students to the shock of an Israeli visitor. A large part of the syllabus in their four-year BA course is devoted to the study of one foreign language. This is an indication of the very limited knowledge of foreign languages, even amongst Chinese university graduates and professionals, as well as the difficulties of teaching and learning European languages for the Chinese. During my stay in Beijing, none of the more than half dozen senior officers in the West Asian and North African Department spoke English; but many of them spoke Arabic and, in one or two cases, French. The only area studies at the college covered the United States and the Soviet bloc. At the time, there was consideration of introducing South East Asian studies. To my hopeful queries concerning their receptiveness to outside lecturers, they told me that only their own Foreign Ministry personnel supplemented the work of the permanent teaching faculty of the college.

The late spring has, in recent years, been an annual period of special tension in China–US relations, and this year was no exception. The renewal of Most Favoured Nation terms of trade for China's exports to the US, reciprocated by China with regard to its US imports, came up for decision in Washington DC early each summer. The inevitable Congressional and media attention and demands for imposing human rights and other conditions on renewal started up in the early spring. The US media and Congress appear to be far more preoccupied with allegations of human rights abuses in China than in any other country. This may be due to the activities and lobbying of Chinese dissidents in the United States. The Chinese are certainly particularly sensitive to such allegations, considering them to be unwarranted intervention in their own internal affairs, and even merely slanderous calumnies, exploited in order to promote US economic interests, improperly and unfairly, at China's expense.

In the midst of this annual controversy, the first top-level Chinese visit to Moscow since the Mao 1957 visit attracted international speculation. Was the visit of Party General Secretary Jiang Zemin, accompanied by the Ministers of Defence and Foreign Affairs, to be viewed as a signal that China now had new international options, precluded during over 30 years of Sino-Soviet tensions and rivalries, in which the armed clashes across the Ussuri River had been the low point? In fact, the rapprochement had begun prior to Tiananmen and the ensuing anger and hostility in the west, with its renewed and invigorated concentration on China's human rights practices and record.

The Gorbachev visit to China, planned much earlier, had taken place during the actual disturbances, in May 1989. It was to be viewed as a logical development in Sino-Soviet relations, stemming from China's policy of opening up to the outside world, from its new economic and trade policies, as well as from the transformations in Eastern Europe and the Soviet Union, which had immeasurably reduced the perceived Soviet military threat to China. The Chinese are realistically aware of the fact that their vital interests in commerce and technological exchanges with the west cannot be insulated from periodic shocks, arising from US 'hegemonism' or the differences in political systems and values; nor do they delude themselves that a Sino-Soviet rapprochement could today have a moderating effect on such differences and shocks. The new chapter in Sino-Soviet relations had nothing to do with China's relations with the west but with the great waves of change in eastern Europe during the previous couple of years, as in China, itself, over the previous decade.

It was certainly a changed situation, in which a Chinese preferential commodity loan and a short term loan in the form of goods to the USSR were announced, and 40 tons of Chinese candy were brought by General Secretary Jiang as a gift to Soviet children. Border problems were played down. They were being examined and resolved, it was stated, in negotiations between the two sides. At the welcoming dinner in the Kremlin, Jiang did not omit mention of the threats of hegemonism and power politics, and of the Sino-Soviet special commonality of interests against the west, in their view of the disparity of wealth between North and South, and the need to establish a new world political and economic order to remedy this disparity, rather than the new world order envisaged or to be imposed by the west. But his stress was on social stability, economic prosperity and unity, and their implicit interconnection

and significance for the future of the USSR, for which China had
the same basic aspiration as for itself, namely the maintenance of
strong central authority and unity. This had become China's crucial
interest in the Soviet Union at that historic juncture, anxious as
China was concerning stability along its sensitive borders, the
continued stability and unity of the USSR and the potentially
damaging example of their breakdown for China's more remote
provinces and minorities, many of which shared close, historic cross-
border ties of kinship, language and culture.

6

From an evening at the theatre to Beihai Park

CHINESE-LANGUAGE readers for foreign students usually include a lesson entitled 'an evening at the theatre'. Like all other aspects of China, the textbook lesson and preparation are a pale shadow of reality. This particular evening was a musical event, held in the Capital Gymnasium. There were over 30,000 spectators, or concert-goers, seated along the tiers encircling a vast amphitheatre. It was like a cup-final soccer crowd, except that older people and parents with small children intermingled with the omnipresent youth of China. Everyone seemed to be eating and/or drinking, the dominant food aroma being garlic. It was a festive, cultural occasion for the masses, at the equivalent of 80 cents (US) per ticket, and most of the tickets had been purchased by the work units (*danwei*) and distributed to their employees.

In the vast centre of the arena were seated three full, separate orchestras, the musicians formally attired in black dinner jackets and black bow-ties or long, black evening gowns. At the appointed time, three conductors together, clad in evening dress and white tie, made their bows. All three orchestras played simultaneously under their three conductors' batons – fortunately, the same piece of music. At the sound of the first strains of a popular Suppé overture or the much beloved 'Land of Hope and Glory', a peal of excitement rose up from the crowded tiers. The first bars of excerpts from *Carmen* and a Tchaikovsky concerto were greeted with booming 'oohs' and 'aahs', and at the first luscious sounds of the 'Blue Danube' and the 'Polovtsian Dances' spontaneous applause reverberated around the arena. This is the western music much beloved by the toiling masses and tens of millions of Chinese.

The atmosphere was completely relaxed, with 'little emperors' and young adults darting off into the aisles, sucking and chewing betwixt and between the melodious strains and movements. The gigantic roars of applause at the end of each piece were received by the conductors with hands clenched above their heads, like champion boxers in the ring. There were six conductors, and they changed places and strutted in and out with confusing frequency and seeming disorder.

Half way through the evening, the garlic odours had merged into a grandiose cloud of fog, interpenetrating with the sweet cloy of the music and acting like a powerful opiate on the audience, in the enclosed arena. The June heat had long before enveloped the entire scene, and all it could now do was to intensify. Our party detached sticky trouser seats and skirts from the wooden tier, waded through mounds of empty drink cans and candy wrappings, and as we gulped air, descending the outside steps, the strains of 'Pomp and Circumstance' aptly wafted out of the arena behind us. It was, indeed, a grandiose, Chinese-scale 'Prom'.

Returning to our apartment building, we moved into the total blackness of a neighbourhood electricity cut, not infrequent in Beijing. But the word 'total' is inaccurate. Our apartment building and the nearby hotels were islands of light, with their own electricity generators. Our landlord was a Hong Kong Chinese merchant, who had sold up his shipping business there and come to live and invest in China. His earliest investment was the construction of our apartment building, consisting of 21 apartments on six floors. It was a well-constructed, tidy and neat looking building, surrounded on the outside with cultivated flower beds and bushes, which spilled over into the lobby, with its two elevators.

Carpeted throughout, centrally air-conditioned and heated, the building was serviced by 42 permanent employees, an average of two per apartment. Nearly a dozen of these bore the grand title of 'engineer'. They were entrusted with all repairs, from hanging tenants' pictures on the walls and adjusting television sets to coping with the power cuts and bringing the house generator promptly on tap. There were also outside service agencies, some of which had to appear from Hong Kong at one or two days' notice. But this was rare, and most of the maintenance could be handled efficiently by the local staff.

It was a matter of fixing standards and requirements to which the local staff might not always be accustomed, maintenance of western equipment and standards of foreigners' comforts being problematic, as yet, in China. But where standards are set and insisted upon, hotels are as comfortable and luxurious as anywhere in the west, and office and apartment maintenance can be as satisfactory as their occupants demand. The problem is supervision of the levels of maintenance and staff. As long as the supervisors and managers are experienced expatriate staff, they can ensure the levels they set. But as companies discover that costs can be drastically reduced by replacing overseas staff with local managers, or local staff demand promotion in joint enterprises, problems arise with the maintenance of standards. This, too, is improving, as local management familiarizes itself with foreigners' requirements and is prepared to insist on local staff satisfying them. But a four-star hotel can become a local hostelry almost overnight, in terms of cleanliness and the functioning of equipment, if management and its levels of maintenance change. The Chinese are very conscious of these realities, as their official policies demonstrate. They have none of the old inhibitions, but only cultural difficulties in learning from the outside world, and its ways and means.

All around our apartments, new buildings were going up at break-neck speed. The labourers living on site in temporary huts, eating collectively prepared food from mess tins, were on the job 12 hours a day, seven days of the week, often continuing to work by search-light late into the night. Within my first year in the apartment, two schools and a municipal office building sprang up around us, their outer structures reaching completion, seemingly entirely the achievement of human labour rather than machinery. The office building was functioning as such before the year was out, and the schools within months thereafter. On a subsequent occasion, I was to escort Chinese guests on a visit to a fully automated factory in Israel, where robot-like carriages moved over a vast factory floor, with scarcely a human within sight. Such a spectacle could only arouse profound anxiety in the minds of Chinese observers, with nightmares of countless millions of unemployed, if their work was to be carried out by machinery and robots.

On my last weekend before leaving for an extended summer home visit and consultations in Jerusalem, I visited Beihai Park in the heart of the city, behind the Forbidden City, on its north-west side. The park covers a vast area, 68 hectares, with a large lake at its centre, on which there is winter skating. Created about seven centuries ago, it is reputed to have been the site of the Great Kublai Khan's Palace, in the thirteenth century. Today, it is a magnificent Chinese Coney Island, playground for the people of Beijing of all ages and a popular attraction for the city's visitors. Hillocks, temples, a soaring White Dagoba, a superb Nine Dragon Screen of coloured, glazed tiles, 5 metres high and 27 metres in length, which scares off the evil spirits on the north-side entrance, lie side by side with children's playgrounds, dodge 'em cars and carousels. The waterside pavilions and covered walkways, barges and row-boats, gardens and rockeries are the essence of Chinese landscape beauty and taste, and a Mecca for the Sunday family outings. Parents and grandparents hover over their precious 'little emperor', urging him to eat ices and candies, non-stop, and the pampered children's reactions are not always in the pattern of the old Chinese discipline and good manners. Dressed up to the gills, the children appear to be the whole purpose of the outing; the 'only child' in China's urban society has become something of a family icon.

The main historic sites and beauty spots have been popularized, girded with rows of food stalls, trinket counters and shops, and adorned with gaudy banners and other decorations. Only the more inaccessible sites, of specialized or archaeological interest, have been spared. The principle being that China's historic sites and beauty spots are for the people, they are prepared and dressed up to appeal to popular tourism and to cater to mass tastes. There is no objective reason why the market atmosphere of the historic sites should detract from their grandeur, any more than the shenanigans in front of some of the great Catholic cathedrals on certain holidays and festivals detract from the piety of worshippers at the shrines within. But they do appear to some to be a kind of popular profanity, even as they contribute to the public recreation and draw people to visit the sites and relics of their national history and culture.

None of the doting families casts an admiring glance at the other children, as do the foreigners. Touring on a public holiday offers the added advantage of being able to watch Chinese families relaxing and interacting. The behaviour of the children in public already offers evidence of enormous changes within the family structure. The very idea of children questioning or resisting their parents' instructions is dissonant in traditional Chinese society and repugnant to Confucianism, which has dominated public and private life and behaviour for millennia, with its strict precepts for the proper management of society and relationship between its elements, thereby ensuring the harmony of society and its universe. Yet today, it is not uncommon to hear parents contrasting their children's values and behaviour with their own, and even admitting that they agree to disagree and to be tolerant of each other's values and tastes. One Chinese friend told me of the harmonious order in his home, whereby he was permitted to listen to his 'repetitive' news broadcasts on radio and television, as long as he did not fuss about his son's favourite pop music shows. Chinese homes have one family room and television set, shared by the generations.

Even more strikingly indicative of the changes was the case of another friend, whose son mocked his lowly government salary and challenged him to go out and earn much more, buying and selling, as did the man's brother. A survey of children in Beijing revealed that the people they most respect are film and pop music stars.[1] Fathers ranked fourth in the survey and mothers fifth. Teachers, most highly ranked on the Confucian scale, were not even in the first ten choices.

Parents whose own youth was wasted in the Cultural Revolution seek single-mindedly the traditional and old-fashioned values of success at school and university entrance for the one and only child. Their natural inclination, even today, is to use old-fashioned forms of discipline, scolding and punishment. Much as they love their children, the Chinese have subtle and non-physical ways of displaying family affections. This does not make life any easier for teenagers, under very considerable school and study pressures, and at the same time subjected to parental demands and expectations in a manner so much at variance with the growing youth culture and aspirations. Despite this, Chinese teenagers can be unexpectedly extrovert. As a study made by the China Youth Development Fund

---

1. 'A New Generation Defies Old Bonds', *China Daily*, 1 July 1993, p. 5.

and the State Science and Technology Commission in 1993 has shown: 'Even middle school students are no longer emotionally reserved.'[2] China's cities and towns are full of Karaoke halls today, and shy-looking Chinese young people get up onto a stage and suddenly display a brashness completely out of keeping with their traditional image and environment. The effects of change on China's children and youth are discernible at Beihai Park any Sunday morning.

My first three months in China were slowly winding down, with my approaching departure for Jerusalem and the tendency for Beijing official activity to begin to taper off after the end of May. The nation's leaders are away in July and August, usually together at the seaside resort of Beidaihe, on the Bohai Bay north-east of Beijing. National policy issues to be raised at upcoming Central Committee or Party Congress meetings or sessions of the National People's Congress in the autumn are thoroughly explored and decisions are taken at these informal summer gatherings. In the absence of the leadership, official Beijing succumbs to the summer heat and lethargy. Foreign ambassadors tend to disappear for a few months, leaving their deputies in charge of the summer doldrums. But city life and bustle continue to be hyperactive. In the public parks and temples, there are constant activities, displays, festivities and cere-monies, with groups of performers from all over China bringing their cultural wares to the capital.

In our official contacts and exchanges, we had made a real start. Channels had been opened up and even formalized. The political dialogue had been fully launched, and cultural relations had moved beyond visiting academics to the first appearance of a Chinese per-forming troupe in Israel. The liaison offices in Tel Aviv and Beijing were functioning over ever wider spheres and were co-ordinating a growing stream of official and semi-official visitors, journalists, provincial and government officials, agriculture delegations, but as yet only a few businessmen. There was still no direct trade between the two countries. In the absence of official relations and commercial agreements, this had not been permitted by the Chinese side. Israeli goods continued to reach China via Hong Kong, and even through

2. Xi Mi, 'Book Shows Great Change Amongst Young', *China Daily*, 5 April 1993, p. 5.

Japanese and other subsidiaries and agencies. Israeli chemical products, pharmaceuticals, computerized systems for printing and publishing, agricultural equipment and animal breeding and improvement techniques were coming into China, to the tune of tens of millions of dollars worth of goods per annum. Chinese exporters were not as interested in the Israeli market, as they had developed no such regular, indirect channels of export to Israel. Two Israeli companies had established small offices in Beijing, run by Hong Kong registered subsidiaries. In any case, goods directly imported into either country would be liable to considerably higher duties and other tariffs and restrictions, in the absence of commercial agreements affording mutually preferential treatment. The normalization of trade had to await the establishment of formal relations, and with them the possibility of negotiating bilateral trade arrangements.

Some effects of the deepening political dialogue between the two countries were discernible in Vice Foreign Minister Yang Fuchang's address at an international conference on the 'Post Gulf War Challenge in the Middle East', held in Vienna at the end of May. The Vice Minister reiterated China's traditional positions on the contents of a solution of the Arab–Israeli problem, restoration of the occupied territories and the legal rights of the Palestinians. These he coupled with respect and assurances for the legal rights of Israel. His approach was not critical or partisan but constructive, customary public Chinese expressions of support for Arab strictures of Israel being notably absent. During the same week, some of the usual Chinese criticisms of Israel's positions were voiced by Politburo Standing Committee member Qiao Shi, on a visit to Damascus, as was to be expected in an Arab capital. But the chief Middle East spokesman and specialist from the Ministry of Foreign Affairs appeared to be carefully avoiding partisanship, at this international meeting as at another, a few days later. This was seemingly further indication of gradual modification of policy, not necessarily precisely co-ordinated up and down the hierarchy, but with the Ministry of Foreign Affairs playing a 'leading role', to use Chinese Communist Party phraseology.

The point of departure of the Vice Minister's comprehensive presentation of China's Middle East policy was that peace and stability in the region and the world at large required the solution of Middle East problems and disputes. He drew three lessons from the Gulf War: (a) interference in other countries' internal affairs and efforts by the strong to subjugate the weak only lead to disaster; (b) political and diplomatic solutions to international disputes and conflicts must become accepted practice; (c) the UN should play a leading role in mediating disputes. These principles had become basic to China's foreign policy and interests in international stability in recent years. Chinese overseas engineering and construction companies had been compelled to stop work throughout much of the Persian Gulf region at the outbreak of hostilities and to repatriate tens of thousands of labourers. Chinese sources estimated the losses sustained by these corporations at more than a billion dollars.[3] This figure did not include a complete assessment of bad debts.

The Vice Minister's position on the UN role served to reassert China's view of its own proper involvement, as a permanent member of the Security Council. Honing in on the Arab–Israeli dispute, which was not labelled the heart and core of the Middle East problem on this occasion, primarily concerned, as it was, with the Gulf War, he called for co-operation by the regional states in arms limitations and destruction of stock-piles, as well as strict prohibition of the use of weapons of large-scale destruction. From Israel's point of view, China's advocacy of direct cooperation and agreement between the parties for arms control arrangements and their implementation, rather than the hitherto fruitless efforts to impose arms controls and limitations from without or by Great Power pressures, was pointing in the right direction. The Latin American Tlatelolco Treaty, worked out amongst the Latin American signatories themselves, is advocated by Israel as a practical and realistic model for regional arms control.

As for efforts to bring about 'a just and lasting peace in the region', the Vice Minister called for bilateral and multilateral consultations and dialogues, as well as a peace conference under the auspices of the UN, and including the five permanent members of the Security Council. This sounded like a modification of the previous stress on the convening of a UN sponsored international conference. It could

3. Ren Kan, 'Li's Visit Viewed as Impetus to Better Ties', *China Daily*, 2 July 1991, p. 2.

appear to give precedence to the goal of a settlement and preference to direct dialogue and consultations of parties concerned, in place of Great Power 'hegemonism', the situation in which the US and USSR were, in fact, sponsors, intermediaries, even initiators. However, it also appeared to signal that China would not be opposed even to that situation, should it be able to facilitate a peace process. The Vice Minister reiterated substantially the same positions at a UN sponsored conference on the Palestine problem, held in Helsinki a few days later (3–5 June).

Sections of the Hong Kong press constitute a primary source for international reporting and rumour-mongering from behind-the-scenes Beijing. Purportedly secret decisions or deliberations of party and governmental inner circles and organs, internal differences of opinion and disputes and leadership rivalries and competition are reported or concocted by well-informed or tendentious correspondents and commentators, collectively known as 'China Watchers'. At this period, one such source reported in a Hong Kong periodical, considered to be politically close to Beijing, the outlines or guidelines for foreign policy cadres, as allegedly laid down by Deng, himself, at a meeting with China's top leaders a couple of months previously.[4] The contents of the report dealt with China's relations with the US and USSR, with Japan, Vietnam and India, with eastern and western Europe, and, fourthly, with South Korea, Israel and South Africa. The latter three countries were, at this period, often grouped together in official Beijing as a single area or unit of responsibility for administration and policy purposes. According to the report, the Chinese leader had stated that:

> Israel should be recognized as a nation and a country. Similarly, the State of Palestine should also be recognized. We recognize Israel. Israel has also adhered to its position of One China. In all the previous disputes at the United Nations over China's legitimate rights, Israel voted in favour of China. In my opinion, diplomatic relations with Israel will be established in the light of the Middle East situation.

4. Cheh Chieh Hung, 'Deng Xiaoping's Recent Talk on China's Diplomatic Line', *Jing Bao*, 167, 10 June 1991, pp. 30–1.

The report added that diplomatic circles in Beijing offered the assessment that formal relations between the two countries were likely 'later this year'.

There was nothing substantially novel in this report. The PRC was formally established in October 1949, over a year later than Israel's independence. By international law and practice, the question arising for a new state, or in some cases, regime, is its own recognition by existing states. They do not require any act of recognition on its part. On the contrary, a new state or regime dispatches a formal announcement, presenting itself to pre-existing states, the official response to which constitutes recognition, on the part of the pre-existing state. Failure to respond signifies non-recognition. The PRC had sent its formal communication to the government of Israel in October 1949, and Israel's official acknowledgement of the communication, on 9 January 1950, constituted recognition of the PRC, as mentioned earlier. China had subsequently neither diplomatic relations nor regular and open official contacts with Israel, but in terms of international practice no question arose of recognition of Israel by the PRC, the establishment of which was subsequent to the establishment of the State of Israel. The statement that diplomatic relations will be established 'in the light of the Middle East situation' was merely a repetition of a Chinese position previously made known to us.

But the authenticity of the entire report can be tested, in retrospect, by the references to South Korea. 'We will never break our promise or abandon our original positions', Deng was quoted as having said, after restating China's position on 'the peaceful reunification programme proposed by the DPRK', and the withdrawal of foreign troops from South Korea. A year later, neither peaceful reunification nor the withdrawal of US forces from South Korea appeared any closer, but China had established full diplomatic relations with South Korea. This could hardly have happened in defiance of Deng, and nothing had occurred between the two countries or in China's relations with the DPRK to bring about a change in Deng's position, if such had, indeed, been his position in the spring of 1991. In any case, authoritative Chinese statements of policy during the months following the report itself, or the earlier meeting, gave no indication of these new or renewed formulations of policy, attributed to Deng.

Before leaving for Jerusalem, I had a *tour d'horizon* with the Departmental Director. We covered the regional peace process and arms supplies and control. I left in his hands my previous proposal for a visit of a couple of our Ministry Departmental Directors in Beijing, for exchanges on the Middle East situation and bilateral relations, as well as a request for their agreement to a visit to Jerusalem of a Beijing opera troupe, to participate in the Israeli (performing arts) Festival, in 1992. This would constitute a second step in visible, cultural exchanges, involving public performances, in addition to the expanding academic, agricultural and scientific exchanges. I was very reluctant to tear myself away from Beijing and the task in hand. But the summer heat and doldrums were already descending upon official activity, and nothing in the way of new visits and exchanges was scheduled or anticipated until the end of July. The process of seeking out and establishing contacts and exchanges had a tempo of its own, which the summer and my departure were setting aside for a while. Beijing is an extraordinarily lively, vital city, with its constant flow of new experiences for the foreigner, and a challenging atmosphere, which it was difficult to abandon, however temporarily, at this particular stage of creating and cultivating a new relationship between the two countries.

7

New nuances and old reassertions

THERE WERE no further developments pending in political contacts between the two countries until the first ever visit of an Israeli Labour Party delegation, as guests of the Chinese Association for International Understanding, due at the beginning of August. On the academic front, visits proceeded in both directions, and a delegation from the Chinese Academy of Science, led by a senior Vice President, were guests of the Israel Academy in Jerusalem in June. For the first time, a formal agreement on exchanges was concluded between the two academies which, in effect, gave expression to the existing contacts and exchanges. On the political front, Premier Li's visit to six Middle East countries, early in July, afforded more insights into evolving Chinese positions on the Middle East dispute, on arms control in the region and, by inference, on attitudes towards Israel.

The visit was presented in the Chinese press as seeking to strengthen unity and co-operation amongst the developing countries, and to exert a positive influence on the process of peace and stability in the region. The designation of these two purposes reflected the two international Chinese policy roles and goals, of Third World leadership and as advocates of international peace and stability. Primary stress was placed upon improving trade links with the countries visited, and the Prime Minister was accompanied by Minister of Foreign Economic Relations and Trade Li Lanqing, as well as by Foreign Minister Qian. China's trade with the Arab Middle East was running at about $1.5 billion annually, less that 0.7 per cent of China's total foreign trade at that period. During the previous decade, Chinese overseas civil engineering and contracting firms had developed lucrative construction business in the region, building roads, factories, hospitals, power stations, oil refineries and residential projects. Following upon the upheavals of the Iran–Iraq War, the Gulf War had compelled these firms to repatriate many thousands of their overseas labourers and sustain heavy financial losses.

More revealing was a summary of the visit in the *Beijing Review*, in which the view was expressed that the Gulf War, while accelerating the Middle East peace process, had weakened the Arab position, Arab unity and especially the PLO, which had sided with Iraq in the conflict. Acknowledging the fact that the United States 'has a bigger say in Middle East affairs' as a result of the conflict, it reported that at a late June symposium on the implications of the Gulf War, sponsored by the Institute of Afro-Asian Studies of Beijing University, opposition had been expressed to the proposed regional peace conference on the Middle East bypassing the United Nations and therefore favouring Israel.

As earlier mentioned, senior Politburo Standing Committee member Qiao Shi, leading a party delegation to Syria, had reiterated China's support for the convening of a Middle East international conference, under UN auspices and with the participation of the five permanent Security Council members, as well as all the parties concerned. He added, for good value, that the Palestine problem is the core of the Middle East problem, and that China steadfastly supports the just struggle of the Arab and Palestinian peoples, and Syria's struggle to regain the Golan Heights. The use of the term 'core' suggests a quasi-ideological or doctrinal commitment or position. He called upon Israel not only to withdraw from the occupied territories, but also 'to change its rigid position and adopt flexible attitudes'. The traditional Chinese hard line on Israel was only to be expected in the context of a party visit to Syria. United Nations' forums, with their extensive Arab and Moslem participation, also continued to elicit the traditional formulations of Chinese policy on the Arab–Israeli dispute. These were not the places to look for subtle changes of policy. During his tour of the region, Premier Li had repeatedly reiterated China's public support for a UN sponsored conference. However, in a reply to a press question, he had confirmed that there were non-governmental exchanges between China and Israel, 'between various organizations in the two countries, in matters such as tourism, science and technology'. This was not the first acknowledgement of such contacts, even in the course of high-level Chinese visits to Arab countries.

In a report of an interview with Foreign Minister Qian in the *People's Daily*,[1] in the course of the visit, the Minister summarized policies in the light of the visit and appended to China's 'consistent stand in the Middle East' the fact that 'China has lately adopted a flexible attitude ... a positive attitude toward any plan which might contribute to peace in the region.' He added, somewhat surprisingly, that 'the most important thing is for the United States, which has a great influence on Israel, to play a greater role.' These comments, carefully phrased as they were, could only indicate China's acceptance of the major US role and initiative in the Middle East peace process, her priority for peaceful solutions rather than for the assertion of a role of her own in the process, and her acquiescence in the subordination of UN auspices to other frameworks. Most interestingly, they indicated that Chinese positions were not monolithic, and that Foreign Minister Qian had an authoritative role and leeway in foreign policy tactics. In this case, the tactics involved an important Chinese UN principle, as well as previous commitments to China's Arab friends, at least on the issue of an international conference and its framework. Premier Li's statements stressed traditional positions and policies, as did those of Politburo member Qiao, while Minister Qian presented the flexibility in policy, a subjection of means to the ends of problem solving and regional stability, which China frequently urges upon others.

New nuances in China's policy on the Arab–Israeli conflict in these early months of the political dialogue between the two countries were very welcome. There were signs that China was departing from a partisan policy of support for the Arab cause against Israel, in favour of problem solving, as consistent with its own larger policy goals and Principles of Peaceful Coexistence with all, including Israel. It appeared to be part of the decade-long process of China's move away from ideology and its slogans, towards pragmatism and an empirical approach in foreign policy.

1. 'China Has Strengthened its Relations With Six Countries', *People's Daily*, 16 June 1991, p. 6.

At this time, consultations were being held in Paris between representatives of the Security Council permanent members on Middle East arms control. Premier Li was reported to have elaborated for his Arab hosts China's 'three point stand' on the subject. The first point called for comprehensiveness and balance, covering all the countries of the region and all weaponry. Regional imbalance must not be further aggravated. The second point dealt with creating a region free from weapons of mass destruction, including nuclear, biological and chemical. Thirdly, arms control needs to be an integral part of the peace process, contributing to the achievement of a just and lasting peace. These were positions to which none could reasonably take exception. From Israel's viewpoint, conventional weapons were clearly covered in the first point. Israel's position was that a start must be made with conventional weapons, all four Israel–Arab wars having been conducted with such weapons. Furthermore, mutual agreement and control (inspection arrangements) are essential, particularly for non-conventional weapons, and China's third point covered the requirement of regional agreement and co-operation.

The visit had served to highlight China's very considerable commercial interests in the Middle East and its stability. It was in the light of these interests that the reluctance of certain official bodies in China to open up direct contacts with our office was to be understood. The Ministry of Foreign Economic Relations and Trade, with its extensive commercial and business links in the Arab world, consistently avoided or evaded our initiatives for direct contacts, presumably viewing such contacts as at best unnecessary, at worst potentially damaging. During the visit, China and Kuwait signed an agreement on Chinese participation, alongside the US and Canada, in extinguishing the burning oil-well fires. Whatever commercial contacts with Israel needed to be handled on an official or semi-official level, such as the visit of the Israel–Asia Chamber of Commerce delegation late in 1990, or the top-level Israeli Chamber of Commerce delegation due to arrive in November 1991, prominent and suitable Chinese business institutions were readily available to play hosts. Early contacts had been made with the powerful China Council for the Promotion of International Trade, as well as with the vast business and financial conglomerate China

International Trade and Investment Corporation. This level of contact was classified in the range of people-to-people exchanges, where Israel belonged from the Chinese point of view, as opposed to governmental contacts, which could come only with formal, official relations.

Before the complete exit of the leadership for the summer, the seventieth anniversary of the foundation of the Chinese Communist Party was celebrated, early in July. It was not an occasion for public, mass rallies, but seemed to be confined to ceremonial party gatherings, prominently featured in the media. The heavy cloud of disintegration of the USSR, and of federal unity in Yugoslavia cast an inevitable pall, so much so that the very celebrations had a ring of Chinese defiance. Public speeches and exhortations were replete with invocations of Marx and Marxist-Leninism. The customary appendage of Maoism was, if anything, downgraded. Slogans such as 'Marxist-Leninism is forever', and assertions that China 'will maintain the People's Democratic Dictatorship, led by the working class', or 'will never turn to a parliamentary type system of the West' had a special strident assertiveness. Socialist modernization and socialism with Chinese characteristics were also proclaimed, but on this anniversary loyalty to the ideology and system abandoned by others was the central theme of the oratory. China had long been moving in pragmatic directions, but it paused from time to time to reiterate the fundamentals of the system. Their evocation tended, unintentionally of course, to raise in many Chinese minds questions of their relevance, in the face of the changes being wrought in society by China's 'second revolution', as the Four Modernizations, opening to the outside world and free market-oriented economic policies were collectively designated.

Party General Secretary Jiang went further in asserting the nature of the regime and political system, in terms of Leninist fundamentals, and referred to 'the counterrevolutionary rebellion which took place in Beijing in the late spring of 1989'. This most sensitive and painful of episodes in the 40 years' history of the People's Republic cannot be brushed under the carpet in Beijing, any more than outside China. The Chinese constantly agonize the whys and wherefores, whether it had been necessary to use so much force to end the demonstrations and whether the situation could have been handled differently from the outset. Outside China, particularly in the west, it was a black and white case of suppression of freedom and brutality, of the image of the lone student facing the oncoming tank. The press and governments in some western countries can be as ideologically committed to the values of their own societies, arising out of their own historical and cultural circumstances, as are Marxist-Leninists. They can also be just as missionary concerning the obligation incumbent upon others to accept their self-evident truths, however varied historic and cultural differences may be.

Chinese friends would tell me how 'un-Chinese' the violent suppression had been, or how unpopular Premier Li was, as the result of his central role in the suppression. This was on the level of Chinese to foreigners, seeking to mollify criticism from outside, despite the fact that violence and suppression have not been uncommon in every culture and in every age. On the thoughtful and serious level, my Chinese friends agonizingly appraised the real implications of such a massive demonstration, and where it could have led. Historically, the Chinese fear anarchy above all else and with good cause. Since the Cultural Revolution, they are highly sensitized to the hazards of mobs of youths in the streets, challenging law and social order. The nightmare was that had the students been allowed to shout down Premier Li at the meeting in the Great Hall of the People, to which he invited them on 18 May 1989, after four Standing Committee members had made the gesture of visiting hunger strikers in two Beijing hospitals earlier in the day, and had they been permitted to defy and humiliate him with impunity, screaming at him that 'this meeting is too late ... the topic of discussion must be decided by us', in front of the television cameras, the reins of government would have been loosened, perhaps irretrievably, authority humbled, and the terrible historical cycle of China falling into chaos might well have been once again set in motion. The accompanying calamities of violence and famines were unthinkable.

China, my friends would often tell me, cannot be ruled by systems imported from abroad. Marxism was adapted and readapted by China's party founders and leaders, and socialism requires 'Chinese characteristics' for local implementation. The Chinese, like many non-western peoples, resent efforts to impose on them western views of human rights and wrongs, much as the west resented and resisted Communist aspirations and efforts to impose its dogmas and systems. They see western individualism, drug addiction, crime rates, atomization of society and breakdown of the nuclear family as inevitable consequences of the removal of societal constraints and discipline, inherent in western views of human rights and democratic freedoms. The Chinese are far from isolated in Asia, in holding these views of western-style democracy.

While western countries felt conscience-bound to punish China after Tiananmen, and US politicians demanded of their administration linkage between terms of trade (Most Favoured Nation arrangements) and human rights, this was no solution to the wide divergences of culture and values, as well as of economic and social realities. Only constant mutual dialogue and exchanges can begin to reconcile such differing backgrounds and circumstances and persuade the parties to seek to make allowances for each other's convictions, cultures and needs – short of conflict and compulsion. China is open to the outside world. She is certainly open to dialogue, but this requires patience. Patience is a great Chinese virtue, to be coupled with gradualness. Both qualities were constantly invoked in the process which was to lead up to diplomatic relations between China and Israel. If the west has faith in its values, it must also believe that an open China, welcoming technology and commerce with the outside world, penetrated by the international hamburger, soft drink and pop music cultures, will eventually embrace patterns of individual freedom, rights and licence, which are the hall-mark of its own societies.

The problem for young, educated Chinese was painfully illustrated by the 'Cultural T-Shirts' episode, which started in the run-up to the seventieth anniversary celebration and continued through the month of July, before being suppressed towards the end of the month. T-shirts bearing slogans or messages considered to be cynical or critical of authority began to be worn by youngsters in the streets. The slogans printed on the shirts read 'Leave me alone', 'Getting rich is all there is', or the Mao slogan 'Do not fear hardship or death', with the addition 'and I'm not afraid of you'. Another Mao slogan on the shirts, 'A single spark can start a prairie fire' was apparently viewed by authority in these circumstances as, at best, ambiguous.

Early in the month, the press reported on the phenomenon, commenting that it was not a bad thing for people to express their feelings on T-shirts, but that some slogans were 'too bad to be accepted'. Some of the unacceptable slogans were quoted, such as 'Nothing can be done, no capital to run a stall, no skill to get into school, no way to become an official, no money to go abroad.' This was described as grey humour, bad for China's image, and counterproductive for China's reform and opening to the outside world. As the month wore on, there was a hardening of official attitudes against the slogans. The manufacturers and retailers of the shirts were issued warnings. Stocks were confiscated, and there were stories of shirts being roughly torn off students' backs in the north west-college neighbourhoods of the city, and of fearful manufacturers burying their stocks in hidden, wooded areas, to avoid being caught with them and punished.

Since the Cultural Revolution, and the periodic demonstrations in Tiananmen of the mid-1980s culminating in the 1989 spring, the authorities and public security agencies are particularly wary of youth fads and activities. The obvious clash of principle in this case was between views of the interests of society and the state, laid down by authority, and the individual's right to express himself, his views and moods. This was a clear illustration of authority ruling against public display of youthful cynicism and criticism. One Beijing newspaper summarized official reaction and positions with the comment that patriotic slogans on T-shirts were fine, but not 'anti-social, unhealthy, shirts'.

In this atmosphere, some felt stifled, deprived of rights of self-expression, in the face of dictates reflecting official views of the needs of over a billion Chinese and the limitations which these must place upon the individual and his behaviour. One mother could tell me at the time that however deeply she missed her only son, studying abroad, she hoped that he would not return to China. A female computer technician expressed herself quite desperately about her yearning to escape what she felt to be a stifling atmosphere, and she persisted in talking about it even after I warned her that the room was probably bugged. But these appeared to represent only a very small number of urban Chinese, their interests and aspirations.

8

Further progress – shocks from Moscow

It was good to return to the bustle of Beijing and the task in hand, even in the humid heat of early July. My first calls were at the Foreign Ministry, where it was by now routine to request and receive an appointment at an appropriate level in the International Organizations Department, where I was instructed to raise matters discussed at the Paris consultations on Middle East arms control, mentioned earlier. The issue of a Nuclear Weapons Free Zone for the region was brought up, and I stressed the requisite of mutual agreement and control by the parties, and also the prior, or at least parallel need to deal with conventional weapons. Far from hedging on the latter point, the Department Director advocated avoiding the creation of imbalances in conventional weapons, and of all sophisticated weapons, as well as scaling down existing stocks.

At a second meeting at the Ministry, in the West Asian and North African Department, reactions were positive concerning the possibility of an acrobatic troupe visiting Israel for the 1992 Israel Festival. We were also assured of their best efforts to facilitate arrangements for the arrival of a Hebrew-language teacher, whom we were bringing to Beijing University to teach a beginners' class. Carefully noting the barometer of these contacts, I was restored to the rank of 'Excellency' and escorted to the front steps by one of my Foreign Ministry hosts, and as far as the entrance hall by the other. It now appeared that they were no longer serious about concealing their official contacts with us from the prying eyes of foreigners, likely to be in the Foreign Ministry courtyard and lobby. Our newly arrived Administrative and Consular Officer paid a call on the Director of the Consular Department the same week. A few days later, the Director of the Division dealing with West Asian and North African Consular Affairs called upon him, in our offices, and later entertained him to lunch, publicly, in the International Club restaurant. The 'step by step' approach was being implemented at various levels.

However, my last meeting with the Department Director, before he took his summer break in mid-July, was a disappointment. It was one of the rare occasions in China when I felt that the step-by-step process could include an occasional step backwards. I had asked for the meeting in order to brief the Department on how we viewed the progress of US Secretary of State Baker's efforts to bring the parties together on the convening of a Middle East peace conference, and on differences of opinion on its scheduling. I was really looking for an appropriate occasion to raise once again what I saw as the next step in official contacts and exchanges between our two Ministries, the proposed visit to Beijing of two Departmental Directors from the Foreign Ministry in Jerusalem. His response to this was that the timing of the visit should be contingent upon the progress in the peace process. Linkage between normalization of relations and progress in the peace process was by now a standard and routine Chinese position. But this was the first time that the development of our *sub rosa* contacts and exchanges, and these not even on a significantly senior level or involving upgrading, was conditioned upon good news from the Middle East or the Washington DC mediation efforts.

Discouraging as this response was after the steady build-up of exchanges over the previous four months, which were cumulatively quite dramatic, there were factors on the international scene to explain demureness or reserve towards Israel at this juncture. The major economic powers, the G7, had earlier in July rejected Israel's request that they call on the Arab states to drop their economic boycott of Israel. Nor was this the moment, so soon after Premier Li's visit to the region, with its promise for the deepening of China's economic ties with the Arab world, for another positive step in Israel's direction. A month was to pass before we were to renew our contacts and initiate the next phase of exchanges, to take place in the autumn.

Quiet as official Beijing becomes in July and August, it remains the place where the foreign policy cadres are to be found, whether these be journalists, on the periphery, furnished with official information and instructions on policy, or foreign policy and intelligence research personnel who summarize situations, developments and recommendations for party and government leaders. These latter have limited knowledge of foreign languages and derive the greater part of their information on foreign affairs and developments from their research personnel, as well as from classified and other news bulletins and reports, often prepared by these same personnel. There are other ill-defined groups of functionaries, often connected with institutes for foreign affairs and contacts, who are assigned or permitted at their own discretion to develop connections with official foreigners and diplomats. During the coming weeks, I was free to concentrate on these contacts. After the initial months of intensive activity, it was useful to be able to discuss and assess where we now stood, how we had progressed and what kind of impact we might be making on our environment.

In a series of conversations at this period, I heard two basic views of our mutual relations, from well-placed sources directly associated with China's Middle East policy research institutions. They were, however, officials or bureaucrats, not 'leaders', the term used to designate the top-level decision-making party and government cadres. These are simply not accessible to foreigners, other than on ceremonial occasions such as official visits from abroad, or formal government receptions. For inside information, therefore, foreigners are dependent upon Chinese journalists, bureaucrats and institutional personnel, and the personal relations of trust which they are able to develop with them.

The first view sounded like an official summary of this stage of our contacts. The point of departure was that there were 'no bilateral differences' with Israel. This was a formulation which we were now hearing not infrequently, and it appeared to be a positive Chinese way of pointing out that our differences and problems were multilateral, arising out of the Middle East situation and China's Arab interests, as well as, certainly at an earlier stage, the complicating factor of the US and Soviet involvements and their spheres of influence and 'hegemonism' in the region. The next point was couched in the same positive tones. Israel's record *vis-à-vis* China placed her in a category of the more friendly countries. This, too, we heard frequently in our official contacts, with our hosts citing Israel's January 1950 act of recognition, her constant 'One China' policy, and her support for China's assumption of her place in the General Assembly and Security Council in the autumn of 1971. Then came the rub. China's overriding priority and policy in the region has been and continues to be to secure her wider Middle East interests. This referred not only to China's economic ties with the Arab states, but also to her concern for peace and stability, and inferentially to her contacts with Israel, in the light of what these could contribute to the process of peace and stabilization. While there was nothing new to us in this formulation, it came from a number of sources and clearly constituted an agreed summation and rationale guiding Chinese policy implementation. Above all, it was void of any undertones of the polemics, criticism or identification with one party to the dispute, which had characterized China's earlier positions.

Another source told me about a 1986 internal policy paper, recommending a change in China–Israel relations. It argued that the absence of relations or political contacts with Israel detracted from China's capacity to play an ongoing role in the Middle East, even from her very pertinence for the Arab world. Lack of contact with one party to the dispute creates an incapacity to exert influence. The Soviets, in the absence of relations with Israel, could ensure their own relevance and role by providing Arab states with aid, arms, training and the very considerable political and diplomatic support of the Communist bloc. China was no longer offering even training facilities to the PLO, as she had during the Cultural Revolution. She was not in a position to be a major arms donor, nor could or would she offer credit and cut prices on the Soviet pattern and scale. Many other countries, which had full relations with all parties in the region, were able to play a far more active and influential role.

Moreover, this policy paper had argued, China's interests in the United States would be served by establishing contacts with Israel. China was very aware of the special relationship between the United States and Israel, and of Israel's standing and support in Washington DC. The Chinese side raised this relationship in every informal and comprehensive discussion of our mutual interests and problems.

The myth of Israel's support and influence in the west in general and the US in particular, was very powerful throughout China. The Chinese view of the relationship of world Jewry with Israel was similar to that of their own kinship with the Overseas Chinese, and they were profoundly impressed by the achievements and status of Jews in western societies. This was a policy paper of the kind that was read and commented on in writing in the margins, according to the source, and circulated in such a way that the leadership received copies containing the margin comments of their colleagues. The comments were generally favourable, if cautious, and they were summarized in the familiar penmanship of one very prominent leader, who penned just four characters, to the effect that the time had not yet come for such a change – '*hai bushi dang*'. However, the subsequent agreement of the Chinese Foreign Minister to a first-ever meeting with Israel Foreign Minister Peres at the General Assembly session in 1987 had been viewed by this source as a major indication of a cautious beginning of change of policy, agreed upon by the leadership, in the spirit of that policy paper, and endorsed by paramount leader Deng.

All the people I talked with at this time were agreed that China's subsequent decision in 1989, that it was no longer too early to start to move cautiously forward in contacts with Israel, resulted solely from the public changes in PLO positions, and particularly Arafat's declaration at Geneva in December 1988, intimating the acceptance of Israel and recognition of the fact that a solution of the Palestine problem would have to be negotiated with Israel, together with the subsequent endorsement of these positions at an Arab summit meeting. If Arafat was ready for contacts with Israel, there was no valid reason for China to hold back and continue to accept the limitation imposed upon her own influence and role by the absence of contacts with Israel. The general conclusion was that the key factor in future relations with Israel would continue to be the Arab–Israeli complex and its resolution. The response to my ingenuous queries in these discussions, as to what our friends would advise us to do, on our own initiative, in order to influence developments, was that we should continue fostering contacts exactly as we had been doing, and that Israel display flexibility in her positions in the peace process.

My first meeting with the Head of the International Department of the *People's Daily* was in mid-July. I extended a formal invitation for one of their senior journalists to visit Israel as our guest. I was told that this would be premature. He added that their Cairo correspondent and a colleague had previously 'passed through Israel', quite unofficially. I mentioned the several New China News Agency visits. His response was that the *People's Daily* is quite different. Its status derives from the Party, of which it is the official organ. In the course of this conversation, I was surprised to learn that just as in Israel, Ministers sometimes called the editor, seeking publicity and coverage; and even when they are courteously rebuffed, they are careful not to take offence or damage their relations with the newspaper.

The beginning of the process of Yugoslavia's disintegration and Slovenia's aspirations to self-determination and independence, with Croatia not far behind, were scantily reported in the media, dryly and factually, without comment or explanation. My Chinese interlocutors expressed grave concern. They were unhappy, too, at the support and sympathy for the Slovenes in some western countries. This they viewed as intervention in internal Yugoslav affairs. In addition to anxieties about Tibet and the provinces of remote western China, one of my Chinese friends posed the hypothetical question of a Taiwanese independence party winning elections and advocating two Chinas. Would European countries and the US meddle in China's vital internal matters, by taking positions in support of such an act of defiance of China's sovereignty and territorial integrity? These were expressions of profound Chinese anxieties, Taiwan and the 'One China' policy being the most sensitive national issue in China today.

The first Israel Labour Party delegation to come to China arrived in Beijing at the beginning of August. Its hosts were the Chinese Association for International Understanding, formally a nongovernmental people-to-people organization, responsible for fostering ties with foreign political parties and groups in countries with which China has no formal relations, and with non-Communist parties elsewhere. Apparently a front organization of the Party International Liaison Department, most of its officials and honorary officers being associated with the Department, this organization had, in the past, hosted visits of members of Israel's Communist and United Workers' Party (Mapam, a party to the left of the Labour Party). The formalities of our contacts on this level were stressed by the host Association members, at the dinner which I gave in honour of hosts and guests. In their speeches, toasts and during the table-talk serenades, the Association hosts extolled Jewish antiquity and achievements, as well as Israel's good record *vis-à-vis* China and consequent prospects for future co-operation. But it was made clear that the framework was people-to-people, that their role as hosts to the delegation was non-governmental, and that I, the host of the evening, represented the Israel Academy of Sciences and Humanities, just as they, the hosts for the visit, represented a people-to-people organization. Like the *People's Daily*, Party organizations were amongst the most cautious in observing the formalities in their contacts with us, although there was no lack of hospitality, courtesy and friendship on the personal level.

If the above-mentioned framework and rules were important for the hosts, what was significant for us was that half a dozen functionaries of Israel's Labour Party were being received in Beijing for the first time, by a Vice Premier, a Vice Foreign Minister and a Vice Chairman of the National People's Congress Standing Committee. Only three months earlier, an Israeli parliamentary delegation had passed through Beijing, on its way to an Inter Parliamentary Union meeting in Pyongyang, and our approaches at the time to the National People's Congress had produced contact only with officials of the NPC bureaucracy, not with members of the Congress itself. The difference between the two cases was that a party delegation can be viewed not as official or governmental, as is a parliamentary delegation, but can be classified in the people-to-people category, and hosted by a formal Chinese host organization, responsible for the visit and the programme. In all such cases, the Chinese people-to-people hosts would arrange meetings for their visitors at appropriate official levels, as had occurred in cases of previous Israeli Communist Party and United Workers' Party delegations.

Whatever the ratiocination and rules of the game, and despite the fact that nothing of the visit or the high-level meetings was publicly announced or reported in the Chinese media, the visit constituted a widening and deepening of China–Israel contacts and exchanges.

Nothing new was said at the various discussions. Knesset member Lova Eliav, leader of the delegation, asked about the prospects for diplomatic relations and normalization and was told that it was a matter of time, and that such visits as that of his delegation contribute to mutual exchanges and serve the process of normalization.

During these weeks of diplomatic activity and intensive efforts in Washington DC, the Middle East and Moscow to achieve agreement on the framework and participation in a Middle East peace conference, the Chinese were closely following US Secretary of State Baker's tours of the capitals and were receiving reports, particularly from the US and the Soviets. Their own reactions were cautious. In all their contacts with us, their support of the peace process and the successful convening of a conference was to the fore. Following Prime Minister Shamir's announcement that Israel would participate in the international conference framework proposed by Secretary Baker, the Foreign Ministry spokesman in Beijing stated on 5 August, in reply to a press conference question, that China welcomed all efforts to promote a peace process for the Middle East and hoped that the Israeli government would take more flexible positions, in order to facilitate the achievement of a just and comprehensive solution. The latter element served to balance China's expression of support for a proposed framework which in fact excluded direct PLO participation and was subject to strong reservations in parts of the Arab world.

This statement was not reported in China, although developments in the multilateral contacts, orchestrated by the US State Department and co-ordinated with Moscow, were factually carried in the media. A *China Daily* headline read 'Baker optimistic on Middle East Talks', and there were no hints of Chinese dissatisfaction with the US role and the side-lining of the United Nations and Security Council. The *People's Daily*, on the other hand, in a prominently featured report from its Cairo correspondent was gloomy about prospects for the convening of a conference and critical of Israel, in keeping with the conservative tone of the newspaper. It stressed Israel's obduracy and the obstacles being raised, particularly with regard to Palestinian participation. It went so far as to question Israel's sincerity in agreeing to a conference, suggesting that she had been pressured into agreement and was therefore creating the obstacles and difficulties. This kind of sharply critical comment was limited to the *People's Daily* at this period.

Ten days later, when Department Director Wang returned from leave and gave me the green light for the visit of the two Department Heads from the Foreign Ministry in Jerusalem, his close questioning on the prospects for the conference and his urging of the need for flexibility reflected the interests and anxieties of Chinese policy, rather than partisanship and criticism, which looked to the past rather than the evolving present and future Chinese attitudes on the Arab–Israeli dispute and the incipient peace process.

The good tidings were that the Ministry was now prepared to schedule the visit of our two colleagues from Jerusalem, but that they were formally to be my guests, arriving at my invitation, not that of the Ministry. Meetings and working sessions with them would be held in the Foreign Ministry, and the Department would offer the customary hospitality, escorting the visitors to the tourist sites and tendering a dinner in their honour. There could be various explanations for the timing of their agreement to the visit. My colleagues saw it as coming on the heels of our final agreement, in mid-August, on all the details of status, privileges and immunities of the two offices. This was the view of the step-by-step approach, whereby the Chinese required one step to be completed and implemented before the next step was embarked upon. My own assessment was that the developments in negotiations for convening a Middle East peace conference and Israel's announcement of her participation in the proposed international conference were much more relevant. Furthermore, a visit to Beijing of PLO 'Foreign Minister' Kaddumi had been scheduled for the end of August. This could now be balanced with our proposed visit in September. This kind of balancing has characterized subsequent official, high-level Israeli visits to Beijing, whether of Israel's President, Prime Minister or Foreign Minister. Each such visit has been preceded or followed by a similar level PLO visit.

China's mass media scarcely batted an eyelid at what one western newspaper headlined as 'Three days that shook the world'. The August 1991 *coup d'état* against Gorbachev, Yeltsin's resistance and the collapse of the attempted putsch, which riveted international attention and dominated the media hour by hour, were relegated to

third and fourth items on the local television evening newscasts, and
to inside pages of the daily newspapers. If they shook any levels of
government and power in Beijing, no one was owning up to it.
Nothing of the mass demonstrations against the coup appeared on
China's television screens or in press photographs, nor of Soviet
leaders being toppled, replaced and taken into custody. Very much
more media prominence was given even to the visit of the Foreign
Minister of the Comoros Islands, and to events in Yugoslavia. This
was a classic instance of Chinese official caution, holding back to
see what should actually develop, before the leadership formulates
its pronouncements or guidelines. On the day after Gorbachev's
release and his historic press conference, the Soviet Union did not
even rate a mention in the midday news, which featured developments in India–Pakistan relations, while the events in Moscow were
reverberating throughout the world and monopolizing the mass
media elsewhere.

In fact, the Chinese media had reduced the Moscow drama to a
non-event. Developments were reported after considerable delay,
of up to two days, and even then selectively, dryly and succinctly,
with appointments and replacements of the leadership presented
without comment, as routine personnel changes. But with foreign
newspapers readily available in Beijing hotels and shops, and with
CNN displayed on screens even in the lobbies of some public
buildings in the city, the two-step flow of communication was more
like wild-fire, and hundreds of millions of radios throughout China
were tuned in to the BBC and VOA.

The Chinese are an extremely aware and curious people, and
news of this kind excites widespread, popular attention and debate.
Enveloping it in an aura of surreptitiousness only adds to the
excitement and speculation. From one Chinese friend I heard an
inaccurate comparison of the positions taken by Libya, Iraq and the
PLO in favour of the hard-line Moscow rebels, and the allegation
that the real sympathies of the Chinese leadership were with the
same group. China is again isolated in the world, he told me, this
time with Arab pariah states. Arabs and Moslems are not popular
in China's streets and market places, regardless of official policies.
His comments illustrated how freely foreign broadcasts are
followed. A couple of others commented to me on the fortunate

circumstance that the students were off campus, on summer vacation. In fact, it was more than unlikely that China's materialistic student generation of the early 1990s would have reacted with anything beyond the same lively interest evinced elsewhere in the cities and towns. There was certainly no hint or glimmer in the local media of Gorbachev declaring that he bared his head before the young people 'who gave their lives heroically to prevent the ascendancy of totalitarian tyranny'.

The stern measures against the Communist Party decreed by the Soviet government on 25 August were not even reported in China, that day or the next. The evening television newscast, which starts at 7 p.m., delayed till 7.25 p.m. the item of news that there had been a shift of power in the USSR and showed Yeltsin instructing Gorbachev to read out to parliament the minutes of the Soviet cabinet meeting. These events had occurred two days previously, and they were relegated to the tail-end of the news bulletin. The measures adopted against the Communist Party were now reported, the following day, with brief quotations from the Tass announcement of three days earlier. The independence declarations of eight republics, breaking away from the USSR, was not announced as such. But it was reported that Yeltsin supported the independence aspirations of the Baltic republics. Eventually, all was reported, but selectively, piecemeal, gradually and cautiously, over a period of several days.

The only official statement eventually issued defined these developments as internal affairs of the Soviet Union, expressed China's expectations of continuing friendly relations between the two countries and asserted China's determination to adhere to its own socialist path of economic development and non-interference. Rumours flew, as invariably on such momentous occasions, in the city's alleys and informal channels of communication (*xiao dau xiaoxi*). There were reports of Deng being ousted, of flare-ups in Qinghai province and in Hui (Moslem) areas, but these stemmed from excited imagination rather than from any signs of unrest or even popular positions of approval or disapproval. In private conversations, Chinese officialdom had never concealed its dissatisfaction with the policies of perestroika and glasnost, and apprehensions were now freely expressed at Yeltsin's approval of decentralization and, in fact, dissolution.

Sino-Soviet relations had certainly improved since Gorbachev's rise to power, despite China's anxieties at developments inside the USSR. In May 1991, Party General Secretary Jiang had made the first top-level Chinese visit to Moscow in 20 years, following the Gorbachev visit to Beijing in May 1989. Tensions between the countries had considerably eased, to the extent of some troop withdrawals from the borders. New co-operation agreements had been concluded, and cross-border trade was rapidly growing. In fact, the developments within the USSR, the effects of reform and the weakening of Soviet unity and power were removing what China had viewed for three decades as the major threat to her security. At the same time, they were substituting the dire and dangerous example of the collapse of socialism and disintegration of the USSR In its own media, the Chinese government could only play down the example, with all its hazardous implications for the regime and system.

9

Hong Kong – Tokyo – New York

Our offices were located down a back corridor in the Jianguo Hotel, the first of the modern tourist hotels to be opened in Beijing in the early 1980s. They were comfortable, conveniently and centrally located, but definitely low-profile. For some time, I had been pressing Jerusalem to authorize the budget to move the offices to a high-profile location, in the China World Trade Center building. We had been negotiating with the building management and at one point had tested official waters by soliciting Ministry of Foreign Affairs help and intervention. In this way, we ensured that any official opposition to the move would precede and obviate a financial commitment on our part. In the latter part of August, the Foreign Ministry in Jerusalem agreed to the very considerable financial outlay of leasing and constructing the floor space in accordance with our potential requirements. The final, key question posed from Jerusalem was whether I could justify such expenditure for an academic liaison office, or were we anticipating and planning for an Embassy within a reasonable time span. My response was that this move was an essential part of our endeavours to become an Embassy, and – more rashly – that in my view, we could now think in terms of six months for diplomatic relations to come within sight, rather than the vaguer year or two, which had been our previous assessment of pace and progress towards the ultimate goal. This was, therefore, the appropriate time to establish ourselves in suitable and visible office accommodation.

The move was authorized. We signed a contract, work was begun, and within three and a half months we were able to move into very adequate and suitable office space, in the most public and prestigious of Beijing's new office complexes. In fact, we manned our new offices just over a month before the official visit to China of Israel's Deputy Prime Minister and Foreign Minister David Levy, and he was able to unveil the Embassy of Israel plaque outside the new offices.

The lull in official activity in August had allowed me to get away for a few days to Hong Kong, where classified reports could be cabled to Jerusalem from our Consulate General. Confidential instructions and information also awaited me there. This was not possible for us in Beijing, where we did not yet enjoy the immunities and privileges necessary to protect our classified material and communications.

Hong Kong is the world's great shopping Mecca. The tourists swarm in and infest the shops and warehouses. Lovely wooded and green areas are to be found on the smaller islands, at the back of Victoria, and in the New Territories. The climb to Victoria peak is deceptively beautiful, so near and yet so far from the man-made squalor below. The overpowering heat and humidity of August bring up the worst from the shallow drainage system. Garbage was strewn and heaped along all but the smartest shopping streets, adding its own vapours to the humid air. The outer walls of the seedy-looking apartment blocks in the residential areas bear the brunt of the harsh sun and tropical rains. Parts of the colony on a hot summer's eve take on the appearance of a vast garbage heap of human waste, out of which rear up the massed, concrete stalagmites that are Hong Kong's architecture.

The sole function of the feverish activity of the city is buying and selling. Rackets and techniques of deception abound. Many of these are born and bred in Hong Kong. Some of the cafes in the modern, smart business blocks have their own system of deceit. A price list in giant print lures by-passers in for a sandwich at the equivalent of two US dollars and coffee at fifty cents. You are billed for four to five times more. The advertised prices, you are now told, are for take-away service alone.

Hong Kong's famous bird-market is symbolic of the city. A long, narrow and crowded lane, stifling and stench-ridden, it is girded along its length and breadth with cages of all sizes, imprisoning thousands of tiny, twittering creatures. The other item for sale in the lane were bags of live locusts or dark-brown crickets, fluttering awkwardly inside nylon bags, mercifully with breathing holes in the nylon. Occasionally, a locust escapes and lands on a passer-by's shirt, hoping to be borne away to freedom. I did not inquire about the propinquity of birds and locusts, but together they seemed to embody the crowded constriction of Hong Kong.

If you get caught up in a traffic jam in Beijing, there is all the time in the world, and patience to match the aeons of history which preceded the motor vehicle. In Hong Kong, the tension is immediate. Your cab driver will be hopping around, trying to manoeuvre in and out amongst his crowded neighbours, all the time broadcasting, nervously, into his communication system, to some distant, anonymous interlocutor. Like so many others, he is too busy anticipating the end of your sentence or request, or too much in a hurry to move on to his own nowhere, to hear you out and respond.

We drove into the New Territories on a Sunday, enjoying the lush vegetation and superb mountain views, looking down upon the panoramas of sea, bays and islets. The shady picnic sites, wooded groves and inviting hiking-trails should have been swarming with week-end escapees from the crowded urban sprawl. They were empty. When we returned to Kowloon, we found that neither shops nor shoppers were having a day of rest. The noise and traffic were unabating. Trees and small public gardens only seemed to sharpen the harsh contrast between Hong Kong's culture of commerce and the good earth, abused for its fulfilment. The Governor's Residence is an impressive, colonial-style residence and park, looking down over the slickest and sleekest shopping and banking areas of Central district. Here are to be found the newest skyscrapers, jammed full with shops, boutiques and restaurants. The offices on the upper floors would appear almost redundant. One of these housed our Consulate General.

Departing from Hong Kong airport, through what must surely have been at that time the world's most crowded cattle-market for long-suffering air travellers, the duty free liquor racket capped them all. It was well nigh impossible to find a poor man's bottle of scotch. Every bottle within sight, on the mobile stalls as in the shopping areas, is several decades old and priced accordingly exorbitantly. I did find one ordinary bottle of gin, at an ordinary price, hidden away on the lowest, floor-level shelf, and the cashier displayed her disdain. China's decision-makers should consider the option of tearing down the whole artificial shrine of capitalism and materialism, when they take over in 1997. The kindest and most humane ecological act would be to let it all revert to Mother Nature. But they are as materialistic as the rest of the world and will contemplate no such inanity or altruism.

It was a relief to get back to Beijing, where the summer was equally hot and sultry, but the people and pagodas so much more real. In the streets, the folk were munching, strolling, cycling or sitting outside their houses, engaged in a variety of outdoor activities and in games mysterious to the uninitiated. At leafy corners and kerb-sides, various exercises were being performed, and other body disciplines, relieving tensions. People buy and sell in China, too, but they retain an old-fashioned, native dignity of movement and behaviour.

A week after returning to Beijing, I was still trying to shake off a bout of Hong Kong influenza, the worst ever to have stricken me down, utterly impervious to the anti-flu shot I had received the previous autumn. In the summer heat, Hong Kong air-conditioning is as harsh as its entire environment, seeking to convert tropical summer into Arctic winter. Dressed for the outdoor furnace, inside the stores one shivers with the man-made cold. When a shop door opens onto the street, a blast of grossly over air-conditioned ventilation lashes out at passing bodies. To this I attributed my Hong Kong flu. Even the air conditioning in Beijing was refreshingly normal.

At the beginning of September, I gave another luncheon in my apartment for West Asian and North African Department colleagues, in honour of a Division Head who had always been kindly, cordial and ever ready to assist us. We saw in him a true friend of the China–Israel rapprochement. He had now been appointed Ambassador to one of the countries of our region. I presented him with a copy of a *Political Dictionary of the Arab World*, compiled by a retired Israeli colleague, who had served as Ambassador in Myanmar. His dictionary had once been espied by a visiting foreign diplomat on the book shelves of a senior official in an Arab state Foreign Ministry. At this luncheon, I heard again, on the official level, explicit linkage between progress in the peace process and normalization of China–Israel relations, as I heard the same week from my most highly placed contact in the State Council (equivalent of UK cabinet office) bureaucracy. This was to become a repetitive element in discussions with our Chinese hosts in the coming weeks and months, but it was in fact being rapidly overtaken by the dynamics of the escalating political exchanges and visits, on their inevitable course to official relations. The peace talks in Madrid, which were to commence at the end of October, were certainly to prove a crucial factor. But the slow progress in those talks could by no means keep pace with the dynamics which were to lead, in just a few more months of brisk activity in our bilateral exchanges, to the decision to establish diplomatic relations. However slow the progress, China's goal was to participate and play a role in the peace conference process and framework – not to be excluded by the lack of relations with a major party to the dispute.

The Israel United Workers' Party delegation, the second of its kind to visit China, arrived at the beginning of September, as guests of the same people-to-people association which had hosted the Israel Labour Party delegation a month earlier. The only difference in programme was that two Communist Party personalities hosted the guests at separate banquets, the Head of the International Liaison Department and a member of its Advisory Council. For us, the difference was that on this occasion, my Israeli Foreign Ministry colleague and assistant at our Liaison Office and I received our first-ever invitations from official Communist Party hosts, to participate in both banquets.

On the morning of the first, a luncheon given by the Head of the Department, my secretary received an unusual and un-Chinese telephone message, to the effect that the invitations to my assistant and myself had been issued in error. No polite excuses were offered. It was made clear that in view of our formal status and that of the Liaison Office, we should not have been invited to an official function, hosted by the CPC. The tone was regretful and apologetic. As if to soften the blow, no mention was made of the following day's luncheon, hosted by a Party Adviser to the Department, for which our invitations remained intact. This was characteristically Chinese. A little inconsistency was allowed, to soften an unpleasant message, which had to be clear but not driven home with a battering-ram. We were both very disappointed and not a little offended. At this time, our progress and success were measured by such steps as these. To be invited and hosted by party Department Head Zhu Liang, a considerable figure in the hierarchy of the party bureaucracy, would certainly have constituted a further breakthrough in our official contacts. The course of good sense and cool heads required us to reconcile ourselves to the setback and be content with the contacts to be made at the second luncheon. In the event, our hosts later demonstrated their appreciation of the fact that we abstained from pointless protest and avoided further embarrassment, accepting the error and its correction. The cadres involved belonged to the party International Liaison Department, and we were, thereafter, to enjoy very cordial relations and useful exchanges with them.

My participation in the meeting of the delegation with Vice Foreign Minister Yang was, by now, routine. Our contacts with the Ministry of Foreign Affairs were being constantly expanded. They were still, formally, secret. Our constant efforts were to extend such contacts to other official organs of government. At this meeting, my position was like that of an ambassador, escorting an official delegation to visit the Vice Minister, with the latter appearing to go out of his way to refer to me as 'your government's permanent representative here, with whom we hold regular exchanges in political matters'. In his concluding remarks, the Vice Minister expressed satisfaction that I would be able to report to my government the views and positions on the Middle East problems, which he had presented to the delegation. These included expression of China's support for all international efforts to promote the peace process (in contrast with earlier emphases on a conference under UN auspices), and of satisfaction with the growing bilateral agricultural and technological exchanges, and with the co-operation between the Ministry and our Beijing Liaison Office.

The contacts with the Ministry were, indeed, cause for satisfaction. We were expanding our discussions into areas of UN activity and of our problems with the specialized agencies. Our contacts with the Ministry's International Organizations Department were now spilling over into contacts between our permanent representatives and Chinese delegates to the UN agencies and meetings in

Geneva, Paris and elsewhere. Our people were pursuing with their Chinese counterparts matters raised by us in Beijing, very often with the same Chinese Foreign Ministry personnel, with whom we had initiated discussions in Beijing. He or she would subsequently attend the conference or meeting abroad, being responsible for the specific agenda item which we had raised in Beijing. In one such case at this period, relating to Israel's efforts to join the Economic Commission for Europe, we were assured that China's decision to abstain, rather than oppose, was taken only after considerable internal discussion and was to be viewed as, in fact, accession to our request. It was scarcely to be expected that at this early stage, China would be reversing or even substantially attenuating her long-standing positions of support for Arab and PLO positions in international forums. This would require very much more time and patient efforts of friendly persuasion, accompanied by favourable developments in the Middle East dispute.

The need to send confidential despatches and information to Jerusalem prior to the planned meeting of the two Foreign Ministers at the UN General Assembly opening session, and in connection with the visit to Beijing of the Israel Foreign Ministry Departmental Heads, took me on a brief trip to Tokyo and the communications facilities of our Embassy there. The contrast between Beijing and Tokyo can only induce shudders of apprehension at what might well become of rapidly modernizing Beijing, visually, in another decade.

When I mentioned to a colleague in Beijing that I was off to Tokyo for a few days, he advised me to take the train straight to Kyoto from the airport, and not to bother to go into Tokyo at all. I thought he was being frivolous. He was not. Tokyo has nothing for the senti-mental journeyer. Even its shrines have a sterilized look about them, with a Buddhism which, after China, appears unoriental, and a Shintoism where you carefully leave your umbrella, together with the shoes, outside on the steps. The elaborate arrangements one finds everywhere to avoid umbrellas dripping from the myriads of plastic brolleys available, for free use, at entrances and exits are typical of the eccentricities which make up contemporary Tokyo. It is urban par excellence, with hyperactivity substituting for soul, sanitation plus tidiness for character and atmosphere. Outside the city, the foreigners' constant complaint is of dirt, refuse and litter abounding in beauty spots and public lavatories alike. Such is the artificiality of the place.

Japanese English, especially in the service sector, is awful, far worse than in China. They pass you on from one incomprehension to the other, without batting an eyelid. At a hotel with which our Embassy has worked for years, and where a room had been reserved for me, they were unable to let my cab driver know the Embassy address. It required too much ingenuity to think of telephoning, or looking the address up in the telephone directory, or to devise any other original means of discovery. The overmanning and labour intensive aspect of whatever the tourist encounters, from hotel front desk to shops, from street repairs to tower attendants and airport facilities may well belong to the Orient but are somewhat unexpected in Japan.

Amongst murkier sides in evidence, the Yasukuni shrine in Tokyo commemorates the dead in Japan's wars, particularly World War Two. Suicide rockets are exhibited, as well as other unsavoury mementoes. A vastly imposing museum and the huge but largely inaccessible Shinto shrine at its side are visited by veterans and the young alike, paying tribute of a personal but also national nature. There is a tendency in Japan to stress Japanese sufferings in war and to disregard culpability and brutality, Japan as victim not of her own doings but of others, and of calamitous weaponry. No hint is to be found of Japanese cruelty, nothing to indicate why even the tolerant and benevolent Dutch cannot rid themselves of their memories and loathing for Japan.

The Japanese have their own brand of memories, cast in their own image, which others have every right to find offensive. A news story in the press while I was there read that, 'the country's first public museum fully covering Japan's wartime aggression will open next week in Osaka.' The museum director found it necessary to insist to the press that 'the truth of the war can be correctly conveyed only by introducing the two aspects of Japan, as aggressor and as victim.' Meanwhile, Japanese continue to flock to Yasukuni, to honour their heroic dead and their deeds, including the ashes of executed war criminals, particularly at the two annual memorial festivals, when prominent politicians elbow each other aside to have their own 'personal' and unofficial appearances covered by the media and cameras. There is some inhibition, presumably arising out of international considerations, concerning openly official participation in these ceremonies of celebration and memorial.

In public life, I was told, it has been a practice to invite opponents or business contacts to play Mah Jong, for cash stakes, sometimes in order 'to learn about the real character of your opponent', but often and blatantly to bribe him with the winnings. This happens in politics, with the government party at times able to neutralize opposition on certain issues on which they wish to avoid public debate, merely by the stratagem of government party members playing Mah Jong with opposition colleagues and losing adequately. The Communists in political life were said to reject this phenomenon of Japanese society. If the Communists could see its faults, the foreigner asks himself, why do others participate in practices which could be viewed as corrupt?

The problem is one of values, culture and of relativism, a product of the west. These same dilemmas arise over attitudes to human rights in China. China's Premier Li holds these to be 'in the first place the rights of existence and development in a vast country with a population of more than one billion', by which he means authoritarian maintenance of order, strict discipline and centralized control and government. The question is at what point do we abandon cultural and value relativism and commit ourselves to an insistence upon our own values, and even to their imposition upon others. Or at what point are we betraying these and ourselves by showing understanding for diversity in cultures, values and human rights?

On a Sunday morning departure from Tokyo, there are endless traffic jams as early as 6.30 a.m. on the thoroughway to Narita airport. The 65 kilometre drive from city centre to Narita airport takes 1 hour and 45 minutes, on an average busy day. Back in Beijing for the Jewish New Year, prayers were held in the private courtyard of a foreign, Jewish merchant family. A few score foreign diplomats, journalists and students were present, including participants in an international Pugwash Conference meeting in Beijing. These included a retired Soviet Jewish General, who revealed that he had never before participated in a Jewish religious service. These may well have been the first New Year and Yom Kippur (Day of Atonement) services ever to be held in Beijing. But Kaifeng, where the only tangible memorials are to be found of the historic Jewish community in China, was represented at the service by a family of Kaifeng origin, residing in Beijing and retaining memory of its Jewish ancestry.

The item pending on the agenda of China–Israel contacts was the annual meeting of our Foreign Ministers at the UN General Assembly session in New York. The United Nations and its agencies serve a purpose of bringing into proximity representatives of states which have no bilateral relations, and which, otherwise, might have no points of contact with each other. Such contacts can prove useful and are, at times, essential. It has not always been the most comfortable experience for an Israeli diplomat to find himself seated, in alphabetical order, alongside a delegate of Iran or Iraq. Not only were the customary smiles and handshakes replaced by a perceptible chill of hostility, but the Arab neighbour's speech or statement to the gathering would invariably include an onslaught on Israel, even when the topic under discussion was non-political and entirely unrelated to Middle East problems. It was sometimes suggested that at least we were hearing each other's viewpoints – if either side was ever listening.

In the case of China and Israel, the General Assembly had served since 1987 to bring together the two Foreign Ministers for their only official contact of any kind. It was at these meetings that agreement had been reached on the opening of the unofficial offices in Beijing and Tel-Aviv, and on exchanges of language students, apart from the comprehensive discussions on Middle East problems, at the highest level. This year's meeting was scheduled for the last week of September. It had in previous years been arranged through contacts between the permanent delegations to the UN in New York. This year, I had initially raised the matter in mid-August, at the Foreign Ministry in Beijing, and they had confirmed that their Minister would be in New York at the same time as our own, at the end of September, and that he would be happy to meet with our Minister again. It was suggested that our UN delegation contact theirs to fix a time.

The meeting was held soon after the opening of the General Assembly. Both Ministers expressed satisfaction at the growing contacts and exchanges of visits, which had ensued from their previous annual meetings and decisions. The Israeli Minister stressed the usefulness of the visits which had taken place, as well as the forthcoming visit to Beijing of the two departmental heads from the Foreign Ministry in Jerusalem. These visits provided important opportunities to discuss Middle East regional problems and the peace process, as well as to promote bilateral relations and exchanges. His Chinese counterpart spoke of China's interest in peace and stability in the Middle East, and in the success of the peace process. China, he stated, was the only Security Council permanent member which has no selfish, narrow national interests in the region but seeks only a fair and just peace, with its benefits for all concerned. She would support whatever steps were likely to promote progress towards agreement and peace between the parties.

The Israeli Minister summarized the situation in the multilateral efforts to convene a peace conference during the coming months. In this context, he stressed the importance of limitations on arms supplies to the region on the one hand, and of establishing multi-lateral and multinational groups to initiate and promote regional development projects in areas such as water resources, agriculture and communications. The Israeli Minister also expressed the hope that China would lend her full weight to the efforts under way to rescind General Assembly Resolution 3379, equating Zionism with racism. The Chinese Minister expressed agreement that the matter required attention and revision but averred that many improper and unjust resolutions had been adopted by the United Nations in the past, some of them anti-Chinese, and that their amendment or suspension was a matter of timing and patience. As for China's position, he pointed out that for some considerable time the term Zionism had no longer been employed in the public formulations of China's policies, and that this would continue to be so. The contrast was with China's repeated condemnations of Zionism over the years, in unison with those of the other Communist bloc and the Moslem countries, and its public designation of Israel as the Zionist entity. He added that China has positions of principle on the Middle East dispute, and he expressed the hope that this was understood by Israel.

The two Ministers agreed that their permanent United Nations representatives would remain in contact on the matter of Resolution

3379, and that they would, themselves, continue their exchanges through their offices in Beijing and Tel-Aviv, through direct exchanges of Notes, when deemed appropriate and necessary, and through the working visits of delegations, such as the Israeli Foreign Ministry visitors shortly expected in Beijing.

This meeting served to routinize the contacts established as a relationship which was, in fact, moving towards normalization. My presence, at my Minister's side, further indicated this process, although it arose out of the need to make a point about my status. In any case, I found it useful in my future official contacts, both with the Chinese personnel accompanying Minister Qian at the meeting and amongst other Foreign Ministry personnel, with whom my daily contacts in Beijing were conducted, and for whom my presence at the meeting had served as further acceptance and recognition of my own status as Jerusalem's official envoy.

The atmosphere of the meeting had been positive and cordial. This was compared and contrasted by my New York colleagues with a coolness and reserve felt at the previous meetings of the Ministers. Not only could it be sensed that previous estrangement and unfamiliarity were replaced by a warm, working relationship and encounter, but the contents of the discussion concentrated on the positive, avoiding unnecessary disagreement. Minister Qian had stressed China's interest in peaceful settlement and wish to be supportive of all moves conducive thereto. He had singled out the fact that the two Ministers had 'raised the level of the functions of the existing liaison offices', as cause for mutual satisfaction, even as he added, without specifying, that we should look forward to further development of relations. The Israeli Minister had been more than responsive, and his invitation to his Chinese colleague to visit Israel, however hypothetical it may have sounded at the time, in the absence of official relations, was neither ignored nor courteously declined. Minister Qian expressed his wish to visit Israel, adding that timing must be a major consideration. On his return to Beijing, a week or so later, China's Foreign Minister made another gesture, by receiving a delegation of the World Jewish Congress. No Jewish delegation had previously been received at so high a level in Beijing.

A few days later, Foreign Minister Qian delivered his opening address to the General Assembly. On the one hand, he reiterated

China's public positions that 'the occupied Arab territories should be returned' and 'the legitimate national rights of the Palestinian People restored'. He called for 'the convocation of an international peace conference at an appropriate time, under the auspices of the United Nations and with the participation of the five permanent members of the Security Council, including the PLO,' but adding China's support for 'all kinds of efforts made by the parties concerned in that region, as they deem appropriate and useful to accelerating the Middle East process'. This was further Chinese blessing for United States and Soviet efforts to convene a conference, not necessarily under UN auspices, which were relegated or deferred to 'an appropriate time'. This was certainly balanced by a call to the international community 'to endeavour to help stop Israel's activities in establishing Jewish settlements in the occupied territories and suppressing the Palestinian inhabitants'.

Minister Qian's concluding call for mutual recognition between the State of Palestine and Israel was further illustration of those Chinese 'positions of principle on the Middle East dispute' mentioned at the meeting of the two Foreign Ministers. Where progress was being made was in the subordination of China's 'positions of principle', its traditional support of Arab positions and the PLO, to the priority of the need for a peace process and a fair and just settlement, without necessarily restricting the means of progress towards these. For the first time, the *People's Daily* reported the bare fact of the meeting of the Foreign Ministers in New York. It added neither explanations that the circumstances were those of China's Security Council status and responsibilities, rather than bilateral, nor commentary on the content or significance of the meeting. It chose to present this item of news in a routine manner, to its Chinese readers and whichever foreign observers might notice it and report back. The act and manner of official publication were not accidental or ingenuous, as the subsequent method of publication of the forthcoming visit from Jerusalem would indicate.

10

Formal ties imminent

The Deputy Director General for Asia and Africa from the Foreign Ministry in Jerusalem and the Head of the Ministry's Centre for Political Research arrived in Beijing at the beginning of October. Before the talks at the Chinese Foreign Ministry, we arranged meetings for them with contacts from the media and foreign affairs research agencies. As long as such meetings were restricted to official Chinese organizations and their personnel, there was no danger of leaks or publicity. Apart from this introduction to the local scene and culture of dialogue, they learned how our local friends and contacts viewed current bilateral exchanges and assessed their future development. On the question of the time span for achieving diplomatic relations, the assessments voiced ranged, surprisingly, from one to three years. There appeared to be a persistent gap between the policy being pursued by the Chinese Foreign Ministry and the process of discreet rapprochement on the one hand, and information filtered down and directives issued to other official organs of government, including the press. This would be deliberate, to avoid unnecessary questioning of policy and rocking the boat, as well as stemming from the general discretion and the capacity for compartmentalization of information up and down the hierarchy, as necessary. My Chinese media friends seemed constantly to be basing their assessments of the momentum of bilateral contacts on an original plan or model of stages for the normalization of relations, drawn up in their Ministry of Foreign Affairs earlier in the year. This plan, as related to me by contacts in the research organizations, was staggered over a minimum of a couple of years. But it had clearly been rendered irrelevant and obsolete, as mutual exchanges and developments in the Middle East and the peace process created their own dynamics.

The main three-hour working session took place in the Ministry of Foreign Affairs at the end of the first week of October. Our host, the Department Director who had led the Chinese delegation to Israel in April, formally welcomed 'the guests of the Israeli Liaison Office', adding that in view of the pace of developments in the Middle East, regular meetings of this kind should be held. In response to our analysis of the post-Gulf War Arab world and forecasts of trends and developments in the region, our Chinese colleagues characteristically reverted to the prospects for the convening of the peace conference and Israel's positions on the issues to be raised at the conference. After these were made known to them in general outline, they summarized their own positions as follows: the very fact of the convening of a conference and the participation of the parties was a welcome step forward. The process could only be lengthy, and flexibility and patience would be required of the parties, coupled with courage, vision and a readiness for compromise on vital issues – and for painful concessions. They reiterated their formal positions that an effective UN role would be essential, that the PLO was the recognized and legitimate representative of the Palestinian people and would have to be a party to the deliberations, and that without mutual recognition between Israel and the PLO, there could be no peace settlement. China was deeply concerned with the peace process and with regional peace and stability. She has no narrow or selfish interests in the region, and her sole concern was for a just and fair settlement, which should contribute to international, as well as to regional stability.

This was China's message in meetings with Arab and Palestinian leaders, too, we were told, and China was constantly urging upon them the need for a settlement of the dispute with Israel. This had been done during Premier Li's visit to the region in the summer, and in the talks with PLO leader Farouk Kaddoumi in Beijing, in August. To our comments on the lack of familiarity in China with Israel's viewpoints and positions, and the imbalance and anomaly in the absence of official relations, the hosts responded by agreeing that mutual contacts had been lacking in previous decades, and that it was natural that we should not share an identity of views. What was important was that there be mutual respect, and that no side should seek to impose its views and positions. Our Chinese hosts expressed the view that there had been considerable bilateral progress in recent months, as evidenced by the exchanges of visits and by the significant extension of political contacts, in Beijing and in Jerusalem. Normalization of relations was only a matter of time, they concluded.

We expressed dissatisfaction at the lack of commercial contacts at the official level. Our hosts assured us that our requests for such contacts were now being considered by the appropriate Ministry, but for the time being they recommended full utilization of the existing commercial channels. They also referred to Israel's restrictions on imports from China and expressed the hope that these be removed. Other bilateral issues were discussed, ranging from cultural exchanges to regional arms supplies. On the latter issue, our hosts quoted previous denials of their Ministry spokesman of press reports of Chinese arms supplies to the region.

The following day, Vice Foreign Minister Yang received the delegation and expressed satisfaction at the significant progress in mutual exchanges and relations. He added his voice to China's urgings that Israel talk directly with the PLO, in view of what he described as moderations in PLO positions on Israel. China's policy is not support for one side or the other, he averred, but for the cause of a peace settlement. In its talks with the parties, China raises not only questions of territory and the national rights of the Palestinians, but also of Israel's security and sovereignty. On the normalization of relations, this, he said, was the interest of both of our countries. But while eastern Asians stress gradualness and patience, western Asians tend to expect immediate implementation. For their part, they were constantly reviewing the level and forms of contacts and exchanges, with a view to the promotion and further development of mutual relations. The Vice Minister concluded by expressing China's hope that positive developments and changes in Israel's positions and in the Palestinian camp would prove favourable to the peace process.

The visit fully achieved its purposes. There were no changes in China's positions. This was not to be expected. Nor did it open up new vistas in mutual relations, or expectations for their normalization. Department Director Wang defined the level of our contacts somewhat informally and loosely as *de facto* consular relations. Their contents were more than that. The visit was a further step in normalizing political contact and exchanges, and in pursuing the diplomatic dialogue between the two Foreign Ministries in a positive, collegial atmosphere. I was addressed as Ambassador at the working sessions, and the Vice Minister, who only one month earlier, during the visit of the Israeli Labour Party delegation, had referred to me as 'your representative in Beijing' and 'your government's permanent representative here' now addressed me as Ambassador, at his meeting with my Jerusalem colleagues. But there was one considerable and tangible step forward, beyond our expectations.

Like the meeting of the Foreign Ministers in New York a few weeks earlier, this visit was publicly acknowledged. Despite Chinese insistence over the previous months that it be a secret visit, at least as far as any official contacts were concerned, and despite the remarks at the opening working session stressing the Liaison Office's role as host, on the day of the meeting with Vice Minister Yang I was informed that the Foreign Ministry spokesman, if asked about the visit at his weekly press conference, would confirm that there were such visitors in Beijing, as guests of the Israel Academy of Sciences' Liaison Office, and that during their visit there had been contacts and exchanges of views with Chinese Foreign Ministry officials on the Middle East situation and other international issues. The question was duly posed by one of the journalists and the response was forthcoming. This was the first time that China was confirming official, government-level contacts with Israeli officials in Beijing. The following day, the *People's Daily* followed up with an eight-line news story and headline 'Israeli Officials Recently Visited China', and the Foreign Ministry spokesman was quoted confirming the fact of talks having taken place. It was reported the same morning by the Chinese radio, as first item in the news bulletin, in the English language *China Daily* and in the Xinhua (New China News Agency) news bulletin. This could be viewed as the most significant step forward since the Merhav visit. The Chinese had now 'gone public' for the first time concerning their official, political contacts with Israel and her Foreign Ministry representatives, outside the UN General Assembly framework and its special circumstances.

As a parting gesture, not without its own connotations of cordiality and personal atmosphere, the new Deputy Director of the

West Asian and North African Department came to the airport, early on a Sunday morning, to bid farewell to the Liaison Office's guests, on their departure for Jerusalem.

As of the spring of 1991, the political work of the Liaison Office had become its primary activity, aimed at achieving the original purpose of its establishment, the normalization of relations between the two countries. However, the agricultural and scientific work of the office was constantly expanding, under the guidance of the Director, Dr Joseph Shalhevet. Even prior to the official opening of the office in June 1990, the Director and his wife, who had arrived a couple of months previously, had been actively engaged in establishing academic, scientific and cultural contacts, with the help and guidance of the Chinese Academy of Sciences, which served as formal sponsor and host for the office. They had been ably assisted by Yoel Guilatt, the Jerusalem Foreign Ministry officer who had preceded Shalhevet in Beijing and made the original office and accommodation arrangements.

The manner in which the Office's work had been conducted, without diverging from its academic and scientific mandate and scope, as agreed between the two countries, had created an atmosphere of confidence and trust. This faithful observance of the rules of the game in Beijing, as required by the Chinese hosts, prepared the way for the decision of the two Foreign Ministers at their October 1990 meeting in New York, to take the next step and permit the office to engage in political work, affording it access to the Foreign Ministry. If the political work subsequently took precedence and primacy, its purpose was to achieve a level of relations such as would make possible the fullest official and unofficial range of agricultural, scientific, commercial and other exchanges of substance between the two countries.

A natural starting point for Israel–China exchanges was the very mix of agriculture, science and technology, upon which the Director had concentrated his best efforts from the outset. These areas have very high national priority in the development of post-Mao China, and the Jewish people and Israel are generally viewed by the Chinese as excelling in them. Home to nearly one quarter of the world's population (22–23 per cent), China has only about seven per cent of the available arable land on earth, on which to grow the crops to feed its peoples. China's leaders pin their hopes on science and technology for agricultural and industrial development alike. Israel's reputation in China is that of a young and highly developed technological economy, in which the agricultural sector has achieved outstanding success with the application of advanced technologies, particularly in the field of water utilization and irrigation techniques.

The visit to Israel in June 1991 of a delegation of the Chinese Academy of Sciences, led by a highly distinguished Vice President of the Academy, was a landmark in the development of these exchanges. The Academy falls under the direct authority of the State Council, which is the government and highest organ of state administration. It is, therefore, an academic body of the highest official status. Two years elapsed from the time the invitation was issued, by the Secretary General of the Israel Academy, on a visit to Beijing in May 1989, until this visit could take place. It finally became possible, a full year after the inauguration of the Liaison Office, as a result of the subsequent development of contacts and exchanges and the breakthrough of the initial secret visits of March and April. Even this encounter was marred a little by the publicity in the Israeli press and the contents of interviews given by Israeli officials, using the visit of scientists to prophesy or infer the imminence of full diplomatic relations between Israel and China. Our guests were embarrassed. My own reservations and warnings that the academic nature of the visit should be respected and not 'politicized' or otherwise exploited in the media were brushed aside – in my view by the desire for publicity, rather than out of any calculation of benefit or of creation of new realities by presenting the visit as a harbinger of diplomatic normalization.

The daily scientific and agricultural contacts of the Liaison Office were, in broad principle, subject to authorization on the political level from the Chinese side; but there was much leeway for local activity and initiatives. If the Ministry of Agriculture was at first reluctant to have direct contacts with us, the development of the scope of agricultural contacts with provincial governments and with agricultural institutions and colleges led to fruitful co-operation and exchanges. The despatch of agricultural missions to Israel, with funding from a US foundation, did later lead to direct co-operation with the Ministry of Agriculture, which was certainly interested in

Israel's agricultural technology but, like other institutions in China, had been inhibited in its contacts with us by the long-standing official policy of estrangement and hostility, as well as by relationships and involvements in the Arab countries. In the summer of 1991, a group of 11 agriculturists had left to participate in various courses in Israel, of eight to ten months' duration. A year and a half later, I was to meet one of their number in Urumqi, Xinjiang province, where he worked in an institute for aridity research and farming, and to find in him a fluent young Chinese Hebrew-speaker, in the heart of north central China. During 1990 and 1991, before the establishment of diplomatic relations, about 40 Chinese attended advanced training courses in Israel, in fields ranging from rural planning to surgery. In the early months following the opening of the Liaison Office, it was difficult to find candidates for the courses in Israel. Advance notices and information were sent out to appropriate institutions, but the response was very uneven. During 1991, interest grew rapidly, and the main limitation on numbers of participants was the lack of funding for travel. In all but exceptional cases of technical and development training courses in Israel, participants or their official sponsors are expected to cover travel costs.

Several mobile courses and joint workshops on efficient utilization of water in agriculture and in advanced irrigation techniques were conducted in China, with lecturers and specialists brought from Israel. These were organized in conjunction with the Chinese Ministry of Water Resources, the China Fund for Helping Poor Areas, and other such institutions. The first publication in China of contacts and co-operation between the two countries was in the form of reports of these courses in local agricultural and technical periodicals. The Beijing English-language *China Daily* reported a visit of two Israeli agricultural engineers to a rural area in Hebei province, in order to explore and examine possibilities of advising on irrigation techniques. This report was the first open indication in the Beijing press of China–Israel co-operation of any kind.

The Liaison Office had developed working relationships and exchanges with the State Commission of Science and Technology, the State Commission for Restructuring Economy, one of its senior officials having paid a working visit to Israel during 1991, the State

Administration for Traditional Chinese Medicine, the Ministry of Health, various planning and technological departments of the Beijing Municipality, the Centre for Research and Development of Solar Energy, and countless academic institutions, particularly Beijing University, the Agricultural Engineering University and Qinghua University of Technology. Visiting lecturers from Israel were brought to these campuses, and a variety of contacts and exchanges was established, including the annual exchange of five language students from each country, and a Hebrew Language and Studies course at Beijing University, conducted by a full-time instructor from Israel. The potentiality for these kinds of exchanges was so rich and varied that the only problem was selectivity, in allocating our limited manpower and resources to maximum mutual benefit.

There was a clear correlation between the developing political contacts and ever-increasing openness to the non-political contacts and exchanges. This was particularly perceptible in the attitudes of certain government departments and official institutions, which had at first kept their distance from us but later drew aside their bamboo curtains. Publication of exchanges with Israel in the Chinese press and the *Science and Technological Daily* invariably elicited comments from various local friends and colleagues to the effect that increasing co-operation should henceforth be possible. It surprised us that so many of our contacts took note of the publication of the October visit of the Israel Foreign Ministry personnel and proceeded to assure us of its significance, and of their own expectations for increasing cooperation in every field. We could not have found a more suitable visiting card to present in China than that of learning, science and technology, nor a better foundation upon which to establish and build our future bilateral relations.

With the Middle East Peace Conference definitely scheduled to convene in Madrid in the last week of October, the comment we had heard from Chinese colleagues that normalization of relations was only a matter of time began to sound much less equivocal. Some 10 days before the convening of the conference, China's Foreign Ministry spokesman welcomed it and expressed hopes for its success. Foreign press agencies in Beijing put out reports attributed to an official Chinese source that relations would be normalized and diplomatic relations between China and Israel established within three months. The source was quoted as adding that there had been no real obstacles in the recent past to the establishment of contacts with Israel. The PLO Ambassador to Beijing, asked to comment on these reports, was quoted as saying that the establishment of relations between China and Israel would largely depend on the outcome of the Madrid talks (by implication, not on the influence or intensity of PLO opposition to such a development). Three weeks later, a visiting Israeli delegation of businessmen asked Vice Premier Wu Xueqian about the prospects of normalization, now that the Madrid meetings were proceeding, and they were told that full development of relations was contingent upon a solution to the Arab–Israeli dispute. But by then, there were already other, very substantial straws in the wind, which indicated that the Ministry of Foreign Affairs had received new directives, of which, apparently, Deputy Prime Minister Wu was unaware.

Some time after mid-October, as the opening of the Madrid Conference drew near, the Politburo Standing Committee had held one of its periodic, unpublicized sessions and given the green light to the Minister of Foreign Affairs to establish diplomatic relations, implementation and timing resting with the Minister and his assessment of international developments. This was the highest level, intermittently convening decision-making body, apart from the comparatively rarely convening Politburo itself. At that period, the Party's 'leading groups', such as that entrusted with foreign affairs, had long been overshadowed by the Standing Committee's more regular exercise of authority, so much so that the 'leading groups' were not invariably kept informed of its decisions, as evidenced by the fact that even Vice Premier Wu, a member of the Foreign Affairs Leading Group, was apparently unaware of it. Otherwise, he would have fielded the Israeli businessmen's query quite differently, without revealing that normalization had been decided and, in fact, already embarked upon. The working papers and recommendations placed before the Committee members were those of the foreign affairs research organizations enjoying special access. The most prestigious civilian body amongst these had very recently sent its Middle East experts to Israel, at our initiative. Our information was that their report strongly urged normalization, arguing for a Chinese role and influence in the peace process, even asserting a measure of Arab support or non-opposition to normalization, in order to ensure maximum Chinese involvement, which would not be acceptable to Israel in the absence of diplomatic relations. Military intelligence recommendations could also be assumed to have been favourable, as were those of the other prestigious and influential, relevant research group, based in Shanghai, with which we maintained regular contact.

Three days before the end of October, Department Director Wang called me to the Ministry to inform me that Vice Foreign Minister Yang wished to invite Israel's Deputy Foreign Minister Netanyahu[1] to be his guest in Beijing, for a couple of days between 6 and 10 November. The visit would be open and publicized, with all that such a public visit would signify. This was the decisive step and break-through. However, fully aware as I was of internal political relations in Jerusalem, even within the Foreign Ministry, I tempered the pleasure of my reaction with careful reservations about how involved Netanyahu was in the Madrid proceedings, and I tentatively suggested that our Director General might come. Director Wang did not even react to the proposal but repeated the fact of the invitation to Netanyahu, alluding to its crucial significance and adding that a day or two would suffice, in view of his present involvement with Madrid.

I conveyed this development to Jerusalem in a coded telephone message, in order to ensure secrecy and avoid the inevitable circulation, however limited, of a written communication. The reaction was one of satisfaction and gratification, but it was out of the question, in the Minister's view, to have Netanyahu come. When I sought to press for the Netanyahu visit, in view of its decisive significance for normalization, I was challenged across the Jerusalem-Beijing telephone divide with the irritated question: 'What world are you living in?', implying that I was out of touch with Jerusalem realities. It took a full week for the Ministry to authorize me to repeat my proposal for a visit of the Director General. I did so, adding the alternative suggestion that, under the circumstances, perhaps Vice Foreign Minister Yang could come to Jerusalem. They were clearly

---

1. Israeli Prime Minister, as of June 1996.

disappointed, as we were, by the fact that extraneous factors were overshadowing efforts to take so very significant a step towards normalization of relations. I gathered that they were not briefed by their people in Tel Aviv about relations within the government party, or the impending departure of Netanyahu from the Foreign Ministry, matters of daily gossip and speculation in the Israeli press. However, they agreed to a visit of the Director General, also to be publicized, and they left it to us to propose dates.

A couple of days later we were picking up reports of another visit, a secret visit to end all secret visits from Israel to Beijing. My colleagues and I were being asked, in mysterious, almost conspirational whispers, whether we would be participating in the meetings and banquet at the weekend. We could only deny any complicity and seek enlightenment. Our friends were obviously suspicious of what they took to be our feigned innocence, but they hinted to us that Israel's Defence Minister was arriving, for a top-secret visit. In fact, in the coming days the visiting Minister was photographed at the Great Wall, by an Israeli tourist, a member of a tour-group from Israel who, however taken aback he was to see so familiar an Israeli Minister in China, had the presence of mind to put his camera to good use. Subsequently, the photograph was sold at a not inconsiderable price, breaking the story of the visit. The visitor was said to have stayed at the Diaoyutai, the government guest compound, and one of my Chinese journalist friends claimed to have followed Premier Li from his visit to a guest house occupied by the Moroccan Crown Prince to that occupied by the Israeli Minister. My report of all this to the Foreign Ministry in Jerusalem met with shock and disbelief, even in the Minister's bureau.

The following week, another Israeli Minister met with his Chinese counterpart, at a Food and Agriculture Organization conference in Rome, and this was the first public, official meeting between Ministers of the two countries outside the UN General Assembly 'special arrangement'. It could have been but was not presented as an extension of the special arrangement whereby China, acting in accordance with her UN role and responsibility, met with Israel delegates to the international body. Nor could it have taken place without the decision of the Standing Committee on normalization. The meeting was friendly and business-like. The

Chinese Minister revealed his familiarity with the agricultural exchanges which had already taken place and with the work of the Liaison Office. He proposed the continuation of the ongoing co-operation between his Ministry and our Beijing office, visits of experts and delegations and future contacts in specialized inter-national forums, such as the FAO. Both Ministers welcomed the mutual benefits of such exchanges and cooperation. The Israeli press reported the meeting prominently, quoting from Israeli sources the Chinese Minister as expressing his view that relations would be established between the two countries in the near future.

The Israeli press reported at this juncture (12 November 1991) that Deputy Prime Minister and Foreign Minister David Levy had briefed the Knesset Foreign Affairs and Defence Committee about a pending visit of his Director General to Beijing, 'as an official guest of the Chinese Foreign Ministry'. This was not the most appropriate channel or manner in which to respond to the Chinese invitation. Meetings of Ministers with that committee are confidential. The *Izvestia* correspondent in Beijing picked up the report and asked the Chinese Foreign Ministry spokesman, at his weekly press confer-ence, for a reaction to reports of a pending visit of the Israeli Foreign Ministry Director General, 'in order to prepare for a visit of the Foreign Minister', and about intentions to establish diplomatic relations. The spokesman replied that China did not have diplomatic relations with Israel, and that any developments in that respect would be duly publicized. Two days later, I was informed from Jeru-salem that it was not possible to schedule a visit of the Director General, in view of his preoccupations with the Middle East peace talks. We had come a long way in our contacts with China, patiently and laboriously, and these last-minute snags and obstacles were inexplicable and frustrating. They were certainly not deliberate delaying tactics but had everything to do with internal complications and relations in Jerusalem, not with relations between Jerusalem and Beijing.

I called on Department Director Wang at the Foreign Ministry to tell him that we could not at this time offer dates for a visit of the Director General, but I repeated an invitation to Vice Foreign Minister Yang without, I hope, creating an impression that we were digging our heels in and insisting that they come to Jerusalem rather than our people coming to Beijing. In our informal contacts, my colleagues and I had sought to explain some of the internal complications involved; but the Chinese were clearly finding it very difficult to understand our reactions to their initiative and invitation, with all the significance of these for the normalization of relations. Director Wang did not conceal his disappointment and commented that they saw 'no possibility of progress in the upgrading of relations, without this proposed step'.

US Secretary of State Baker had been in Beijing in mid-November, and the question of China's participation in the peace talks, certainly at the multilateral level, was reported to have been raised, in hypothetical terms. At the weekly Foreign Ministry press conference on 22 November, a Radio Beijing reporter obliged with a question as to whether China would be participating in the next round of the Middle East peace talks. The spokesman replied that if invited, China would consider participation. He added that as a Security Council permanent member, China consistently acted to promote a comprehensive solution of the Middle East dispute, on the basis of the relevant UN resolutions. The Madrid Peace Conference of the previous month had, the reply concluded, constituted a positive step in that direction. This was a very characteristic Chinese way of expressing interest in playing a role in the current process, perhaps constituting a public clarification of the hypothetical question, as reported during the Baker visit. The bilateral process, at this stage revolving around the proposed visit, was not to be divorced from the peace negotiations. China was very aware of the fact that Israel would not welcome nor even countenance the participation of other states, in addition to the Arab parties to the dispute, which did not maintain normal relations with her. The US was playing a role in clarifying to the Chinese that while they were not, themselves, averse to Chinese participation, there were enabling conditions not of US making.

At this time, a high-level Israel Chamber of Commerce delegation was in China, hosted by the China Council for the Promotion of International Trade. For the first time, senior officials of the Ministry of Foreign Economic Relations and Trade met publicly with Israeli visitors. Even more significant from the viewpoint of our status in Beijing was the fact that our colleagues in the Chinese Ministry of

Foreign Affairs let us know in advance that if they were invited to my reception in honour of the delegation, they would attend, allowing themselves for the first time to be seen as our guests, by a cross-section of journalists, diplomats and other foreigners, as well as by our numerous other Chinese guests. Amongst these were senior officials of the Foreign Economic Relations and Trade Ministry mentioned above, which had previously kept its distance from us.

In fact, this was the first such visit to be handled on an official rather than people-to-people basis. All the banquets and receptions were attended by representatives of the Foreign Ministry, the Foreign Economic Relations and Trade Ministry, and other government departments. I was seated on the host's right or left, as the official representative of the visiting delegation's government, and my colleagues at the Liaison Office were also invited, thereby indicating an official status for the office. The delegation, including myself as their government's representative in Beijing, was welcomed by Vice Premier Wu, in the leadership compound of Jungnanhai, 'on behalf of the Government of China'. However, this was the occasion on which the Vice Premier told the delegation that full normalization of relations would depend upon 'a solution to the Arab–Israeli dispute', thereby suggesting from the highest government source a prolonged time span, whereas actual developments were indicating that it was a matter of weeks. An American visitor was similarly told by the Deputy Head of the Communist Party International Liaison Department that her 'personal view' was that progress was required in the peace talks, in order to lead China 'to recognize Israel'. The same visitor was told by Foreign Minister Qian that things were 'on course for a gradual and progressive approach to the ultimate goal of normal relations'.[2]

If things were indeed on course, at this moment the course was barely moving. The delay was explained in a 'personal communication' from Deputy Prime Minister and Foreign Minister Levy to his Chinese counterpart. Recalling their discussion of the peace process at their New York meeting two months previously, and the

---

2. Nicholas D. Kristof, 'China Expects Eventual Ties With Israel', *New York Times International*, 29 November 1991, p. A3.

115

subsequent convening of the conference for the launching of direct negotiations between Israel and her Arab neighbours, he summarized the developments and the current stage of implementation of the Madrid Conference decisions and of convening the bilateral and multilateral meetings agreed upon at Madrid. The Israeli Foreign Ministry's preparations for these talks were the responsibility of the Director General. For this reason, he could not, at this stage, confirm a date for a visit of the Director General to China. In conclusion, the Israeli Minister expressed the hope that the two Ministers might be able to resume their discussions in the near future, and he renewed the invitation to his Chinese colleague to visit Israel, which had previously been proffered at the New York meeting in September. At the same time, the Director General met with the Director of the China International Tourist Service's Israel office, explained the situation to him and repeated the hope that Vice Foreign Minister Yang might be able to come to Israel.

Within the Chinese Foreign Ministry, practical and day-to-day considerations were affecting the tempo. The Foreign Ministry's task is to ensure China's international role, influence and activities. The sponsors of the incipient peace process were two of the Great Powers, and the European Community had also been present at Madrid, in the role of observer. Furthermore, in the planned multilateral forums, which were to deal with a wide range of practical matters, regional water resources, economic cooperation, refugees and environment, it was already envisaged that there would be active participation on the part of all the interested powers. Japan, Canada and the European countries were involved in the discussions and consultations. China had no part in these preparatory activities, and the absence of normal relations with Israel was the inhibiting factor.

China had not sought a major role of sponsorship of the Middle East peace talks, like that of the US and USSR (later, Russia). It had, in fact, given public blessings to the efforts of the sponsors to bring the parties to the dispute to the conference table. However, China clearly supported regional stability and an end to conflicts, which could only damage commercial and business interests. It was the task of the Foreign Ministry to ensure that China's positions were presented and its interests promoted on the international scene in the effective manner appropriate to its international status. There was now a Chinese decision to implement normalization in tandem with the development of the peace process mechanisms, in such a way as to ensure China's proper participation in these. It was counterproductive to fall behind in participation in the process itself, in which so many other international parties were becoming involved and would make their contribution. China's delayed participation could only prove negative for her international standing, including her position in the Middle East and Arab world. Considerations of this kind clearly favoured the case for immediacy in implementing normalization of relations with Israel.

The tempo of bilateral contacts and exchanges was, anyway, indicating imminent normalization. The Israel Chamber of Commerce delegation had been received officially at all levels, and we were being openly treated as a foreign mission for all practical purposes. The previous formal limitations on our activities, and on open contacts with us on the part of a whole range of officialdom had been completely superseded. We had come a long way since the 'misunderstanding' over the invitation of the Head of the Party International Liaison Bureau, only two months earlier. At this time, the Director of the Xinhua, New China News Agency Middle East regional bureau, was received by the Prime Minister in Jerusalem. The Agency comes directly under the State Council. Its personnel are government officials, and the Head of its Middle East Cairo Office is a very senior cadre.[3] This meeting in Jerusalem was reported in the *People's Daily* and by Radio Beijing, in a routine manner. In fact, it was the first official contact in Jerusalem with Chinese governmental representatives to be publicly reported in China. A further indication of change was China's absence from the UN vote, early in December, rescinding the 1975 'Zionism is Racism' Resolution. China had originally supported General Assembly Resolution 3379. A few weeks earlier, in a message to an annual UN International Day of Solidarity with the Palestine people, Premier Li had appended to the customary support for the legitimate national rights of the Palestine people and for the restoration of the occupied Arab territories a statement of the need for the sovereignty and security of Israel to be respected and guaranteed.

---

3. Later appointed a Vice-President of the Agency, in Beijing.

117

This, in a Chinese message to a Palestinian celebration, was later, in retrospect, interpreted as 'a public signal that formal ties with Israel were imminent',[4] although the Chinese Premier had made exactly the same statement in Cairo, early in July, quoting from his own 1989 Five Points for Peace in the Middle East.

4. Lillian Craig Harris, *China Considers the Middle East* (London: I.B. Tauris, 1993), pp.262–3.

11

Culminating visits – no longer so secret

Six weeks had passed since the Chinese invitation for an official visit of the Israel Deputy Foreign Minister, later adjusted to the Director General level, at our request, and we were not yet able to offer dates for a visit. The further and final step prior to normalization was being delayed, somewhat inexplicably in the eyes of our Chinese colleagues. We were well aware of the internal problems at home. The public credit for the normalization of Israel's relations with China could not have been appropriated by the Deputy Minister, nor by a Director General. Much as I tried to explain to Jerusalem by telephone that the final and public step would be taken only at the ministerial level, this was neither understood nor credited. The press reports and photograph of the alleged top-level Israeli visit to Beijing in November had inflamed ministerial sensitivities and rivalries. My only recourse, in these circumstances, was to continue to urge upon our Chinese colleagues the despatch of Vice Foreign Minister Yang to Jerusalem.

Plans for the multilateral level of meetings in the Middle East peace process framework were developing and being discussed in all the major capitals. It was also being made clear to Beijing, in the major capitals as well as by ourselves, that China's involvement, however appropriate and desirable, would require the formality of even-handedness, at least in China's formal relations with the parties to the dispute. At this juncture, I was given a prior hint that in view of the difficulties we were having in scheduling a visit of our Director General, they were trying to rearrange Vice Minister Yang's schedule and obligations. At the same time, we learned of a visit of PLO Chairman Arafat to Beijing, planned for mid-December. Once again, Chinese foreign policy was balancing its act.

On 14 December I was called to the Foreign Ministry and informed that Vice Minister Yang would like to come to Israel the following week, for a discreet visit not to be publicized. The purpose of the visit was to be briefed on the peace process and to discuss bilateral relations. The West Asia and North Africa Department colleagues who conveyed this to me were clearly delighted. For them as for us, this was the long-awaited, decisive step towards the joint goal.

The situation at this point was well summarized in a report which appeared the same day in the Hong Kong *South China Morning Post*, under the headline 'Full Ties With Israel In Sight'. The report quoted diplomatic sources, to the effect that full ties could be established between China and Israel 'as soon as next month', and before the next round of the international peace conference on the Middle East, scheduled for late January. 'Beijing has indicated its eagerness to take part in the conference, and its image of impartiality would be boosted if it were to normalize relations with Tel Aviv before then', a diplomatic source was quoted as saying, adding that 'even Arab countries have pressed Beijing to establish ties with Israel', hoping that the Chinese could use their influence to help them at the peace conference. The report noted that in recent months, Chinese officials had toned down criticism of Israel and highlighted bilateral exchanges. It also quoted extensively from a television interview with Deputy Prime Minister and Foreign Minister Levy (of 12/12/91), in which he, too, held that the two countries were 'marching towards the establishment of diplomatic ties'. He was reported as declaring that he was making preparations to visit Beijing.

This report certainly summarized the directions in which events were moving, and the policy considerations powering them. The journalist, Willy Wo-Lap Lam, had good and long-standing contacts in Beijing. The predictions bore signs of US sources, as well as of his Chinese contacts. The latter, however, had revealed nothing to him of the forthcoming visit to Israel, with its significance for the timing of developments.

I arrived in Jerusalem a couple of days before the visit of Vice Minister Yang, to find considerable irritation in the Foreign Ministry at the Arafat visit to Beijing. Arafat's standing was at a low point, in the Arab countries as on the international scene, following the

Gulf War earlier in the year. He remained *persona non grata* throughout the region, apart from Iraq, the Europeans were holding very much aloof from him, and he no longer had a supportive and sympathetic eastern European bloc to invite him for official and well-publicized visits. Our people thought that this was certainly the wrong time for China to have invited him, and not conducive to the progress of the peace process, from direct participation in which the PLO was excluded, at Israel's insistence.

My task in the Ministry was to make it clear that China's official position was firmly supportive of the PLO, with which China had official relations, and of the political rights of the Palestinians to a statehood with which China had established diplomatic ties three years previously. Some of my colleagues, who felt that their duty obligated them to be more hawkish than the government of the day, received these clarifications of China's policy with the demagogic question of which government I was representing. In our service, it was not unknown at certain periods for ambassadors to be accused of 'going native', when they performed the task of reporting to Jerusalem on uncongenial policies of the countries to which they were accredited. I never had this experience with government Ministers, but there were senior civil servants capable of giving expression to their loyalty and commitment in this manner.

Vice Minister Yang left Beijing for Israel on the day following Arafat's departure from Beijing. The morning of his arrival in Israel, a colleague and I were instructed by the Director General to receive the five-man Chinese delegation at the airport, express Israel's displeasure at the Arafat visit to Beijing 'at a time when he is being ignored by the entire world', and to inform the Vice Minister that we found it necessary, therefore, to publicize the visit. I took a firm position against such a course of behaviour, passions subsided and the Director General agreed to go to the airport and receive his guests in the appropriate manner.

The question of publicizing the visit, which our guests had requested to be kept discreet, had already been taken care of that morning at the meeting of the Knesset (Parliament) Foreign Affairs and Defence Committee, at which the Foreign Minister had confided that Yang was due to arrive. Israel radio announced the fact in its news bulletins, quoting Committee sources.

On arrival, the delegation was escorted to the King David Hotel, in Jerusalem, and a late dinner was scheduled in a small, separate dining room, to discuss the programme for the following days. After the dinner, our guests took leave of us and were the first to go out into the hotel corridor. They turned hastily on their heels and re-entered the room, to our surprise. In the corridor, they had been confronted with a number of journalists and press photographers lying in wait for them. The guests were very taken aback, and only after our insistent pleadings with the press posse, were they allowed to pass. There was no way of explaining to our guests, or to ourselves, how this situation had come about. The usual explanations, of free press and open society, could only sound somewhat offensive under the circumstances: they were, nevertheless, offered. The noteworthy freedom and openness were those with which confidential arrangements and classified information were made available to the press. Our Chinese friends had experience of this in their previous contacts with us. But they continued to be surprised anew, uncomprehending and surely sceptical.

Wherever they went throughout the following three days of this secret visit, the guests were hounded by the press, even at meetings at ministerial level. After the initial experiences, Vice Minister Yang 'confessed' to being in Israel, as a guest of the Israeli office of CITS and its Director, thereby formally publicizing the visit. This explanation was published in Beijing. He urged us, even pleaded with us, to maintain secrecy on the contents of the talks, particularly the arrangements for Deputy Prime Minister and Foreign Minister Levy's visit to Beijing, planned for January, and the communique agreed in advance on the establishment of diplomatic relations. Premature publication could only give the opponents of normalization prior warning, enabling them to rally their forces and exert pressures against these developments. His final words, on the day of his departure, were to express profound regret that everything concerning the visit had appeared in the local press, 'even the contents of my talks with Ministers'.

The Israeli press not only reported what was said and concluded between the two sides, but it coupled the agreement on normalization with the Chinese wish to participate in the multilateral conference on the peace process, due to convene in Moscow on 28

January. Members of the Chinese delegation pointed out that this commentary could only detract from the significance and the essence of the establishment of diplomatic relations between our two countries.

We had planned a detailed and comprehensive agenda for the talks, ranging from the peace process and the Middle East situation, including the thorny problem of arms exports to the region, to cultural and student exchanges and friendship leagues. At the opening working session, Vice Minister Yang announced that the primary purpose of his visit was to consult with his hosts on normalization of relations, and that he was the bearer of a letter of invitation, from his Minister to his Israeli counterpart, to visit China. He proposed that his own visit be utilized for the purpose of preparing the act of normalization of relations, to take place during the Israeli Minister's visit to Beijing. This was the reason for the need for secrecy with regard to his own visit, in order to preclude interference with the arrangements for normalization.

At the meeting with Deputy Prime Minister and Foreign Minister Levy which followed, Vice Minister Yang delivered the letter, and arrangements were agreed for a January visit to Beijing and for the normalization procedures to take place during that visit. The Israeli Minister welcomed new possibilities to expand and develop areas of cooperation, with the establishment of relations. He also briefed his guest on the Madrid and Washington talks between the Arab and Israel parties, and on the multilateral forum to be convened in Moscow at the end of January.

Vice Minister Yang expressed China's full support for the peace process and its deep satisfaction that the parties were now pursuing the path of solution of disputes in the only feasible manner, that of peaceful negotiations. It was clear to China that after 40 years of hostilities, the differences were profound and bitter. He urged patience, flexibility, pragmatism and a practical, realistic approach on all sides. He expounded in detail China's views on the dispute, particularly on the issues of territory, the rights of the Palestinians and Israel's right to security, and he expressed China's sympathy for the Palestinian people and their sufferings. He welcomed the salient and significant development that the parties were now in dialogue and seeking mutually acceptable solutions. He stressed that

China had opposed earlier Arab positions on driving Israel into the sea, just as it had consistently opposed terrorism. It had also supported the right of all the states in the region, including Israel, to their sovereignty and territorial integrity. He concluded this part of his presentation with an expression of hope that Israel might be able to implement some confidence-building measure on the issue that was of particular grievance to the Palestinians, namely settlements in the West Bank and Gaza. He added that this was in no way intended as interference in the policies of other countries, but as an attempt to facilitate dialogue and understanding amongst all concerned parties.

Foreign Minister Levy pointed out that Israel was the first to engage the Palestinians as partners in negotiations on administrative and autonomy concepts for Judea, Samaria and Gaza. No party had ever before involved the Palestinians as partners or offered them autonomy, least of all the Arab states. For Israel, her self-defence capabilities had been crucial over the past 40 years, and these would remain crucial, in order to deter aggression and war and promote peace. For this reason, Israel urges upon all suppliers of weapons and military equipment to the region to desist, thereby giving peace a chance, and with it the historic opportunity to put an end to wars in the region and heal the wounds of the past. In conclusion, the Minister expressed his pleasure at the prospects of his forthcoming visit to China, together with his appreciation of Vice Minister Yang's mission to Israel, in order to arrange the visit. It was later agreed that Minister Levy would arrive in Beijing at the end of the third week of January, from where he could proceed directly to Moscow, for the multilateral conference. It was further agreed that publication of the visit would take place on 12 January.

Vice Minister Yang was probably the most experienced and senior figure in China's Middle East establishment. He visited the northern and eastern borders, saw with his own eyes the problem of the Golan Heights, commanding Eastern and Upper Galilee, and for the first time he was exposed to the complexities of the dispute from the vantage point of Israel. He also saw something of Israel's agriculture and industry. It may have been an unfortunate choice to have him visit one of the country's most highly automated plants. The spectacle of robot machines moving across a vast factory floor, seemingly of their own volition, fetching and carrying, loading and unloading with hardly a pair of human, working hands in sight, was not the most optimistic industrial scenario for a responsible civil servant of a country with the largest labour force in the world, running into several hundreds of millions, of which at any given time over one hundred million casual labourers flooding into the cities from rural areas are unemployed, or at best under-employed. China can produce far more economically with human labour than Israel can with machines, and the stability of its society, as well as its well-being, could depend at this period of its history on avoiding mass unemployment and dismissals from unproductive enterprises. The visitors were very conscious of the irrelevance, even the threat of such sophisticated mechanization to their system and needs.

Half-way through the visit, at the conclusion of the working sessions, the Israeli press and television were reporting details of the talks, complete with photographs and headlines announcing discussions of diplomatic relations, and the invitation to Foreign Minister Levy to visit China. One photograph bore the caption 'Secret Visit in the Eye of the Camera'. It was certainly a well-reported secret visit. During the first week of January, regardless of agreements on dates of publication of the visit and pleas for discretion concerning its purpose, the international press was to follow the Israeli press in reporting the forthcoming visit, clearly stating its purpose.

All the reporting linked the normalization with (Israel's agreement to) Chinese participation in the multilateral conference, due to open in Moscow on 28 January, with the participation of about three dozen countries, to be represented for the most part at Foreign Minister level. This clearly dictated the timing. There were those in China's leadership who had opposed haste and sought more gradualness, while others argued that there was no point in missing out on participation in the international peace process, at a time when neighbouring Tokyo was joining the growing number of capitals being touted as hosts for the various, regional working groups (dealing with water resources, refugees, environment, arms control and economic matters). There is no doubt that leading members of China's foreign policy establishment viewed the time-table for normalization as a process yet to run many months, and conditional upon results in the negotiations process, while others, particularly in the Ministry of Foreign Affairs, felt the time was ripe and the timing right, and these elements were pushing ahead with the process of normalization, furnished with the Standing Committee's authorization.

It is clear that not all policy issues are formulated in detail by the leadership for the administrative branch to implement. Just as there is give and take in the implementation of economic, currency, investment and credit policies, with so-called conservatives pulling in one direction and free-wheeling free marketeers pushing the inflationary spiral ever upwards, until the paramount leader or the Politburo intervene to change or confirm general course, so in the case of normalization of relations with Israel had the green light been given to implement normalization. The tempo of the forward movement to the eventual logical conclusion was in the hands of the Ministry of Foreign Affairs, unless challenged by another government or party agency. The idea of a monolithic decision-making body dictating and monitoring decision-making and implementation at all stages, in a system of democratic centralism, is too theoretical for the realities of the vastness of China and the complexities of its government and administration. There are degrees of informality and leeway in implementation, facilitated by the fact that Ministers are often Politburo members, as is the case with Deputy Prime Minister and Foreign Minister Qian, Vice Ministers may well be Central Committee members and every government department and unit has its own party committee. Those who supervised and guided China's contacts with Israel in Beijing were all members of the CPC, carrying out its policies and decisions, to be deflected only if the manner of implementation was formally challenged and submitted for reconsideration. This was unlikely, but premature leaks and publicity could only alert opposition or questioning of the tempo of events.

At the end of the first week of January, the Israeli press anticipated the official 12 January announcement of the visit and further reported that Foreign Minister Levy would sign on the dotted line in Beijing on 24 January. The BBC spared our blushes somewhat by broadcasting the reaction of the Foreign Ministry spokesman in Jerusalem to these reports, to the effect that information on the visit would be made available in due course. The *Far East Economic Review* was more explicit, reporting that normalization of relations would be announced during the visit. Both these latter reports linked the timing with Chinese participation in the Moscow meeting. The *Far East Economic Review* stressed the Japanese role in the multilateral level of the peace talks as decisive in the timing of Vice Minister Yang's visit and the normalization agreement. Our Chinese friends continued to tell us that this tie-up, between diplomatic relations and participation in the Moscow meeting, was only diminishing the historic significance of the establishment of diplomatic relations between our two countries and belittling the actual extent of bilateral exchanges and the mutual esteem of recent years.

The New Year atmosphere in Beijing was, for us, certainly festive. Our Chinese friends, feigning unawareness of what had not yet been made public in their own country, warmly embraced us with their smiles of joy and felicitation. The Chinese Foreign Ministry personnel, with whom we were in constant contact over the details of the ministerial visit and schedule, shared our emotions and excitement at what was about to be finally accomplished, crowning the joint efforts of the preceding months. The Beijing diplomatic corps, parts of which had cautiously kept their distance from us in the past, now sought us out, as much to express satisfaction with the developments as to seek information and confirmation. Even the Arab Embassies, we were told, had been prepared over a period of time and were not making problems. The PLO Ambassador was said to be acquiescing, in order to ensure China's participation in the Moscow conference. Only the Iranian Embassy was reported as lodging a protest, and we were told of expressions of dissatisfaction from the People's Bureau of the Great Socialist People's Libyan Arab Jamahiriya.

The first Israeli civilian aircraft ever to land at Beijing's Shoudu (Capital) Airport came down on schedule on the morning of 22 January 1992, its markings and pennants reminding us of earlier tussles over the appearance of the Israeli flag in Beijing. The Minister was accompanied by a couple of dozen Israeli journalists, cameramen, television and radio correspondents, seeing China for the first time. The hosts had clearly gone out of their way to ensure the warmest of Chinese hospitality. The Minister and his party were assigned a government guest house usually reserved for heads of state. The winter sun shone brightly over the lakes and trees, the classical Chinese landscape of the Diaoyutai official guest compound, in western Beijing, as the Israeli guests were ushered into a culture and environment with which they were entirely unfamiliar, and the beauty and charms of which can be overwhelming at first exposure.

The Chinese had entertained vegetarian guests not infrequently, but Jewish dietary laws were entirely *terra incognita* for them. A week or two earlier, the wife of the Director of the Liaison Office gave detailed briefings and guidance to the guest house staff and kitchens. It may be that something was lost in translation, as was so often the case in communication in China, but the chef d'oeuvre on the Minister's luncheon table were giant Chinese shrimps, crowning the salad dishes. The staff had been clearly warned that all sea-food was forbidden under Jewish law, and that only fish which had fins and scales was to be served. These restrictions were later to become even more confusing to Chinese hosts, as more and more Israelis came to China, bringing with them each his own selective laws, lore and practices, and in many cases requesting and relishing every form of 'forbidden' food. In this instance, we anxiously invaded the kitchens, to have them put things right. The calm reaction was that there was no cause for concern, these particular shrimps being fresh-water creatures, not sea-food. In our innocence, we were unfamiliar with this subtle distinction, but we finally managed to convince them to make the necessary changes, before the Minister emerged for his first Chinese repast.

The Minister had arrived a day or two early, in order to have an opportunity to visit the sights of Beijing and the Great Wall. He also visited the beautiful old mosque in the Moslem Hui quarter of Niujie, built in classical Chinese style. There he was received by the Imam and other dignitaries of Beijing's Moslem community. While it had been we who requested this visit, from China's view-point it was a demonstration of how Jew and Moslem could come together in China, in a hospitable and friendly atmosphere. It was to provide one of the photographs of the visit published in the world press, featuring smiling visitors and hosts engaged in lively conver-sation in a Beijing mosque courtyard. The mosque and courtyard are one of China's Moslem community's oldest sites, with relics dating back a millennium, and it should find a place on every visitor's list of tourist sites.

Foreign Minister Qian was due back in Beijing from an African tour on the morning of the 24th, the day for which the official talks and the signing of the agreement on the establishment of diplomatic relations were scheduled. The two Ministers had met twice previously, at the United Nations General Assembly in New York. Foreign Minister Qian, whose 18-hour flight from Africa had landed in Beijing an hour or two earlier, warmly greeted his Israeli guest at the Diaoyutai, on Friday morning, 24 January 1992. The occasion was an illustration of the stamina required of today's Foreign Ministers, who traverse continents from one day to the next and must arrive alert in mind and body for the tasks awaiting them. This occasion had its own festive atmosphere, which the two Ministers conspicuously relished.

The Chinese Minister received his guest in the entrance hall of the conference pavilion and escorted him into a smaller meeting room, where the two Ministers held a preliminary discussion, without their delegations. Each expressed satisfaction at the achievement of diplomatic relations, and the Israeli Minister thanked his host for the warmth with which he had been made welcome and the hospitality of the opening days of this first visit to China. He presented his views on the potential for developing mutual relations and co-operation in many fields, as well as on the contribution of their normalization to the international atmosphere in general, and to communication and understanding between nations and peoples. In this latter context, the Israeli Minister reviewed the Middle East peace efforts, and the obstacles created by hostility to peace on the part of radical and fundamentalist regimes, as well as by arms supplies, particularly to the radical regimes which threaten Middle East stability. He urged China to exert her international influence on behalf of the peace process, and against these obstacles and threats to regional stability.

Foreign Minister Qian responded that stability and the peace process in the Middle East were of vital concern to many countries throughout the world, as they are for the peoples of the region. He expressed China's support for the process and his belief that the establishment of relations between China and Israel would prove beneficial to that process. He urged flexibility as the key to progress in the negotiations, and such progress as the best antidote to the negative forces, opposed to peace in the region. At this point, he proposed that the formal ratification of the agreement on the establishment of diplomatic relations take place, in the presence of the two delegations, and thereafter to proceed to the discussions and agenda.

The solemnity of the occasion of the signing by the two Ministers of the Joint Communique of the Government of the State of Israel and the Government of the People's Republic of China on the Establishment of Diplomatic Relations was alleviated somewhat by the champagne, and the personal toasts exchanged between the working-level diplomats on both sides, for whom the occasion was a shared professional and personal fulfilment.

At the working session of the full delegations, it was agreed to examine together potential fields of co-operation, and also the possibility of establishing the framework of a joint commission, headed by the two Foreign Ministers, which should periodically examine and authorize progress and recommendations. Both sides expressed their basic positions on the need for Middle East peace and positive approaches for its promotion. The Israeli Minister again raised the problems of regional fundamentalism and arms supplies. His host reiterated the view that progress in the peace talks was best calculated to weaken the negative influence of fundamentalism on all sides. He stated China's wish to avoid a regional arms race and her participation in international efforts and co-operation to promote a fair arms control agreement for the region. He expressed understanding for Israel's security concerns and condemned terrorism in all its forms, reasserting China's position on the sovereignty of all the states of the region.

This was a carefully balanced presentation of China's positions. It coupled formulations critical of terrorism, fundamentalism and extremism on all sides, and in support of a 'fair and just' regional arms control agreement, with the belief that the historic experience of sufferings of the Jewish people engendered sensitivity for the sufferings of others, and a call for a suitable solution to the territorial problem and the legitimate rights of the Palestine people. It was a more balanced and even-handed presentation than previous Chinese statements, but it was made in the closed forum of a top-level encounter between the two countries. Nevertheless, it was noted that these formulations were very similar to those heard from Israel's traditional friends in the world community. Mention of the Jewish experiences in China, from the early arrivals of a millennium ago up till the Second World War, and of visits of Jewish delegations and their concern with China–Israel relations, demonstrated the Chinese view of the unity of the Jewish people, similar to their view of their own people, at home and overseas. In this respect, the Chinese hold a 'Zionist' view of the Jewish people as a national entity, the home-land of which is Israel.

After the working session, the press was invited to meet the Ministers, and the Joint Communiqué on the establishment of relations was read out. The first two paragraphs contained the decision to establish relations at the ambassadorial level, effective as of 24 January 1992, and a declaration of Israel's recognition that 'the Government of the PRC is the sole legal government representing the whole of China, and Taiwan is an inalienable part of the territory of the PRC'.

The Ministers expressed to the journalists their satisfaction at the establishment of relations, and the Israeli Minister thanked his host for the hospitality and friendly atmosphere in which the discussions had been conducted. Foreign Minister Qian spoke of the importance of bilateral co-operation and China's hopes for the peace process. He announced that China would be represented by Vice Minister Yang at the peace process multilateral talks opening in Moscow on 28 January. To a question on China's role at the Moscow meeting, the Minister pointed out that this would be China's first partici-pation in the peace process, and that its detailed positions would be presented in Moscow. The Israeli Minister was asked how China's arms sales to the region could be reconciled with a positive role in the peace process. He replied that arms sales certainly conflicted with the peace process, and that this pertained not only to China but also to other countries with which Israel has friendly relations. Diplomatic relations and dialogue between the two countries would, he believed, contribute to the reaching of mutual understanding in this, as in other areas.

In the afternoon, the Israeli Minister was whisked to the

Jungnanhai government compound in the official black limousines, now flying the Israeli and Chinese flags. We saw that the flag had also been raised over the villa which we were occupying in the guest compound. We immediately contacted our offices in the China World Trade Center and had them raise the Israeli flag over the building now housing the new Embassy of Israel.

The Minister was received in Jungnanhai by Premier Li Peng, who described the establishment of relations as a landmark in the history of the two peoples. China had always supported Israel's right to existence and statehood, and it was ready to develop normal and friendly relations with all states, on the basis of the Five Principles of Peaceful Coexistence, regardless of differences in social or ideological systems and approaches to international issues. The Israeli Minister expressed his view that the establishment of diplomatic relations was a positive contribution to the peace process, reiterating Israel's anxiety at the growth of fundamentalist tendencies and arms supplies to the region, both of which are liable to impair the peace process. The Premier responded with the hope that the multilateral talks would be productive, that they would be conducted in the spirit of United Nations' resolutions, and that all the parties, especially Israel, would be more flexible and enthusiastic about the process itself. Expressing admiration for the Jewish people and its historic experience, and sympathy for its sufferings, he repeated the theme of understanding for the sufferings of the Palestinians, growing out of the Jewish experience. He made reference to China's long-standing sympathy for the Palestine people and its cause. After taking somewhat less even-handed positions than his Foreign Minister, Premier Li concluded with the comment that differences of opinion should not have a negative influence on the development of friendly relations and co-operation.

Premier Li requested that his greetings and best wishes be transmitted to Prime Minister Shamir, and to Defence Minister Arens 'with whom I have recently met here in Beijing'. Minister Levy responded that a central task for Israel in the bilateral relations would be to seek to persuade the host government of her views and positions, particularly with regard to Israel's peace initiative. He brought greetings from Prime Minister Shamir and from President Herzog, who had expressed to him the wish to visit China in due course, and he invited Premier Li to visit Israel. His host replied that such a visit should be considered at an appropriate time, to be co-ordinated by the two countries.

For Friday evening and the sabbath, the Minister and his closest aides were transferred to the centrally located Grand Hotel, which also flew the Israeli flag for the occasion. His spacious suite of several rooms was a startlingly impressive mini-palace in traditional Chinese decor, as was the landscaped building occupied by the delegation at the Diaoyutai government guest compound, and the Minister's suite there in particular. The move was made because the Minister could not use vehicles on the sabbath but wished to be able to have access to the city on foot. The government guest compound was not within walking distance of the lively, central downtown areas and Tiananmen Square.

On Friday evening, the Minister hosted a traditional sabbath-eve ceremonial dinner at the hotel, attended by close to one hundred guests. There were the official delegation, the accompanying press corps and photographers, the flight crew, the Israeli students in China and the handful of Israelis working in Beijing, together with their families. It was the occasion for the Israelis to celebrate together the first sabbath eve of diplomatic relations between China and Israel. After blessing the sacramental wine, we toasted the special events of that day, in which we had been privileged to participate.

On Sunday, 26 January, the Israeli delegation, journalists and Embassy of Israel – formerly Liaison Office of the Israel Academy of Sciences and Humanities – staff members gathered in the corridor of the fourth floor of the China World Trade Center, West Wing building, outside our offices, together with a few of our close Chinese friends, for a modest, informal and unscheduled ceremony of unveiling the Embassy of Israel plaque. The Minister invited me to stand at his side, and the photographers went to work as he removed the cloth cover, stating simply that this was a moment which Israel had long awaited. It was, indeed, the most moving single moment for the small team of Israelis who had been working in Beijing for normalization from the outset, and for this very transformation of an academic liaison office, situated originally down the recesses of a hotel back corridor, into what had become by late 1991 a *de facto* Embassy in terms of its range of activities, situated in appropriate, high-profile offices. This was now Israel's newly established Beijing Embassy.

From there, we proceeded to our first official reception, in the China World Hotel's grand ballroom, attended by over four hundred Chinese guests, from every level of China's public and national life, as well as from a very wide range of academic and cultural circles. These represented the scope and calibre of the contacts we had made during the comparatively short time which had elapsed since the opening of the Liaison Office, and it was an impressive gathering, upon which we received favourable comments from our guests, and from experienced foreigners, diplomats and 'old China hands'.

The Minister and his party departed the next morning for Moscow. At the airport to see them off were Russia's Ambassador to Beijing and Vice Minister Yang, whose visit to Jerusalem the previous month had signalled what was to come, and who would be meeting the Minister again in Moscow at the opening of the Middle East peace process multilateral conference the following day.

12

The new chapter

The unique estrangement between China, which had been virtually the only non-Moslem and non-Arab country in the world to have eschewed all relations with Israel throughout the four decades of the People's Republic, and Israel, which had sought direct contact with China from time to time and had no bilateral quarrel with her, was ended not by the stroke of a pen, but as the result of a succession of historic, international developments. Chief amongst these were the change of direction in China following the end of the Mao era and the advent of the 'second revolution', with the opening to the outside world, the rise of Gorbachev and the collapse of Soviet Communism, with the ensuing drastic change in the balance of international influence, interests and involvement in the Middle East, and the effects of these upon Arab and PLO options, attitudes and positions, opening up new vistas of negotiations in the Arab–Israeli dispute. The first of these factors had earlier made possible the contacts between China and Israel in the 1980s, and later their evolution and fruition.

The months of unofficial political activity, dialogue and exchanges of visits during 1991 had led to the final step at the year's end. The political activity had been preceded and accompanied by the assiduous and fruitful academic and scientific work of the Liaison Office. This was thought to have earned the confidence of the Chinese hosts that they could rely on us to play the game by the rules. The President of Israel's Academy of Sciences and Humanities at that period and the former Director General of the Foreign Ministry and Consul General in Hong Kong, Reuven Merhav, have both been quoted as stressing the crucial nature of discretion and secrecy for the Chinese in the preliminary contacts and exchanges in which they had been involved in the mid- and late 1980s.[1] This may well have been true of the early years, and of the first months of the functioning of the Liaison Office in Beijing. However, from the moment direct political exchanges began, in the spring of 1991, discretion appeared to have been flung to the winds.

Publicity and leaks to the press dogged every move and contact, however much the Chinese side urged secrecy. Yet, these did not affect developments, nor even their tempo. The Chinese were unconvinced by our lame explanations that such was the nature of a free press and society. One senior official complained that the contents of his secret talks with Israeli Ministers were leaked not by the press, but by senior government figures who had participated in the talks. Another had earlier pointed out that Israel had in the past proved her capacity to maintain secrecy, in her own interests. They were quite certain that the publicity and leaks were deliberate. Yet they did not allow these to impede the course of events.

Furthermore, while policy decisions were made elsewhere, control of the tempo of developments and their management appeared to be firmly in the hands of the Ministry of Foreign Affairs. While it could not always persuade some other government ministries to go along with the development of contacts with Israel, it could determine, itself, when to step up the secret official contacts with Israel and exchanges of visits, and how to handle its parallel contacts with the Arab states and the PLO. It conducted the contacts and exchanges in accordance with a carefully graduated planning concept, which had at its core the need for peace and normality in a stable Middle East, the inception of a Middle East peace process and China's own perceived role and contribution in the peace and regional normalization process.

The flexibility which China constantly urged upon the parties to the Middle East dispute was fully displayed in the manner in which the Foreign Ministry itself conducted its contacts with Israel during 1991. The precedents of the build-up to full relations with the United States a decade previously, and with the Republic of Korea

---

1. Avital Inbar, 'Credibility, Patience, Secrecy – and into China', *Globes*, Tel Aviv, 10 January 1992, p.23.

at the same period as with Israel, could well have given reason to expect a lengthier period of incubation than the 20 months which elapsed between the opening of the Liaison Office and 24 January 1992, or than the nine months following my arrival in Beijing to initiate regular and structured political exchanges. Our own expectations had been in terms of years, similar to the US experience, as were those of our Chinese friends. The Foreign Ministry, and with it the Politburo Standing Committee decision-makers, proved to be more pragmatic and flexible, moving with an agility and control adapted to the development of events in the Middle East, to their own view of their political contribution and role, and to what the Middle East traffic, i.e. their long-standing relations in the Arab world, would bear.

It would appear from the actual handling of events that the original Chinese decisions sanctioning the establishment of the Liaison Office in Beijing and a CITS bureau in Tel Aviv constituted, in fact, the green light for the Foreign Ministry to go ahead and develop relations according to its own assessments of China's interests, subject only to any major questioning or challenge which might be raised en route. It would appear that no serious challenge was raised, but rather that the pace of events was carefully and discreetly prepared, nourished and strengthened by the recommendations and reports of official visitors to Israel during 1991, and particularly of the relevant foreign affairs research institutions, with which we sought to develop close contact from the outset. This was borne out by the fact that senior, and some very senior figures in the political and foreign policy establishment were not aware of the imminence of normalization as late as November and early December, 1991. Their assessments were in terms of China's careful gradualism. In fact, the matter was no longer on their agenda, but in Foreign Ministry hands, for implementation, following authorization of the final step, at the highest level, in late October.

The Foreign Ministry urging for discretion and secrecy surrounding each development and visit may well have been aimed at avoiding challenges or questioning from amongst the staunch old friends and supporters of the Arab world and the PLO in China, including its own 17 million strong Moslem communities. Decision-making in China's democratic centralist system does leave implementation leeway in the hands of the administrative organ of government, at the head of which, in this case, was a State Councillor and Foreign Minister, not yet a member of the Politburo or Deputy Vice Premier. Both these promotions were to come to Qian Qichen in the course of 1992 and 1993, reflecting his previous standing and authority in the party and hierarchy.

The *People's Daily* represented at that period the more conservative factions and views within the Party leadership. Its positions on Israel and the Middle East dispute throughout our early months in Beijing were consistently critical, even hostile from our viewpoint, and had made us feel that as far as attitudes towards Israel in this official organ and bastion of the CPC were concerned, little had changed since the Cultural Revolution. An editorial on 25 January 1992, marking the formalization of relations, heralded the dawn of a new day in the attitudes of the *People's Daily* towards Israel. In keeping with the earlier-mentioned Chinese 'Zionist' concept of the Jewish people, it recited the Jewish nation's diligence, wisdom and contributions to civilization and human progress, followed by expressions of the Chinese people's deep sympathy for the historic sufferings of both the Jews and Arabs. Calling for a just, reasonable and comprehensive Middle East settlement, it urged the return of occupied Arab territory and restoration of the legitimate rights of the Palestinian people. At the same time, it averred, the sovereignty and security of all Middle East countries, including Israel, must be respected and guaranteed. The hope was expressed that all parties concerned would assume a flexible and practical attitude to achieve peace.

There were two clear messages for the public in this editorial. China's public relations with Israel were now on an entirely new footing, with friendly and practical dialogue replacing recrimination and condemnation, and that China's interpretation of Security Council Resolution 242 was unchanged, in support of Palestinian rights, but no more so, as previously suggested, than were many, if not most of Israel's friends in other capitals and governments throughout the world.

In China, gradualism and patience characterize the tenor of interactions and transactions. Deputy Prime Minister and Foreign Minister David Levy had told a reporter during his visit to Beijing that the two countries should now move ahead rapidly and make up for lost time. Before the end of 1992, Israel's President Herzog was to make an official visit to China, as was Foreign Minister Qian to Israel. Commercial, scientific and technological agreements were concluded between the two countries, and a weekly charter flight to Beijing of Israel's national airline, El Al, had been inaugurated. If this did appear to be somewhat accelerated progress, it was the fruit of the labours of those who had come to China a year and more earlier, before normalization, and had toiled in pre-normal conditions to create a solid foundation of contacts, friendships and co-operation, on which to construct the future of relations between China and Israel.

Epilogue

PERUSAL, AT the end of 1996, of a text dealing with the process leading up to the January 1992 establishment of China–Israel diplomatic relations and written in the first year or two of those official relations, suggests the need for an epilogue of assessment of the five years of relations and exchanges.

The establishment of relations grew out of a new era in Middle East and Israeli history, in which negotiations between Israel and her Arab neighbours started slowly, laboriously and, at times, painfully to displace the violence and warfare which had dominated these relations for over 40 years. The incipient process of negotiations was the immediate factor leading to public, official Chinese contacts with Israel. The broader context and background was China's policy of opening up to the outside world. China could play a role in promoting the solution of local disputes through direct contacts between the parties, minimizing as far as possible external great power or 'hegemonist' interference. This has been a basic policy of the Dengist period, with China seeking to contribute to the creation of an international stability in which China's interests in trade, foreign investment and technology transfer could be maximized.

China's policy towards Arab–Israeli negotiations was consistent over the five-year period. Eschewing the previous policy and rhetoric of condemnation of Israel, 'the Zionist entity', and of partisan support for Arab anti-Israel positions and measures, Chinese policy has evolved into constant support for the Middle East peace process, repeatedly urging upon all parties patience and flexibility in the face of the complexities of what, in China's view, must of necessity be protracted and laborious negotiations. Desisting from voicing criticism or apportioning blame, as in the past, China accompanied the ups and downs of the process with expressions of understanding for the 'increasingly complicated and sensitive nature of the question involved', and of the need for 'a flexible and pragmatic approach and persistent efforts' on the part of the parties concerned. These positions did not gloss over China's support for what it considered to be a 'fair and reasonable' or 'just and lasting settlement', namely the restoration of their legitimate national rights to the Palestinian people – without China spelling out the details of such rights. But the overall aim is 'peace, stability and the development of the Middle East region as a whole'.

The even-handedness and balance in the positions over the period was constructive and did not disappoint expectations. Nor did the promise held out by official relations. While China's hopes for the removal of the 'core' problem and cause of Middle East instability has not yet been realized, China has not, until very recently, appeared dissatisfied or impatient with the progress made, and its relations with the parties no longer appeared to be in sharp conflict, as they were in the past. The post-Gulf War Middle East, repairing damage, rebuilding, rehabilitating, continuing to modernize and vary consumption patterns and demands, and to invest resources internationally, offered opportunity to Chinese exports of consumer goods and manpower, as well as import of capital. A Middle East at peace can only enhance such opportunity and potentiality, as well as meeting the needs of China's growing consumption and imports of energy.

Concrete expression to these interests is provided by China's participation in all five multilateral working groups, which followed on from the 1991 Madrid Conference and were inaugurated at the 1992 Moscow Conference, by participation in the Casablanca, Amman and Cairo economic conferences and by China's interest in joining the proposed regional development bank. There were unofficial expressions of dissatisfaction in Beijing at the fact that China was not invited to the March 1996 Conference against terrorism, held at Sharm-el-Sheikh, in Egypt.

However, a disturbing change in China's political tactics, if not in its policy on the peace process, was perceptible in the closing months of 1996. China appeared quite suddenly to revert to a partisan position of, at worst, 'punishing' Israel, at best signalling political displeasure at what China now viewed as tardiness in Israel's implementation of the Cairo and Oslo Israel–Palestinian agreements, particularly on redeployment and withdrawal from the town of Hebron. This expressed itself in a series of sudden cancellations of high- and middle-level Chinese visits to Israel, the chief of which was that of Vice Premier Li Lanqing, scheduled for mid-November 1996. While this and half a dozen other cancellations were publicly explained away, in face-saving terminology, as arising from scheduling problems, it was quite obvious from the timing and succession of cancellations that there was nothing haphazard or fortuitous about their intent and significance. Lower-level official visits and delegations continued to flow, in both directions.

For the Israeli government and those involved in Israel–China relations, this was a disappointing and quite unexpected development, out of keeping, it was felt, with an international image which China has sought to project in recent years, of seeking peaceful solutions to international problems by direct negotiations between the parties, without undue interference and pressures of external 'hegemonist' interests.

This change in China's multilateral, regional tactics on the Israel–Palestinian dispute and peace process will probably prove to be temporary, even an aberration from the norm. It has done nothing to enhance China's influence upon Israel or the peace process; rather has it limited further China's regional role and influence.

In the realm of bilateral relations and expectations, this first half decade following the ending of the Chinese ban on direct trade with Israel and the conclusion of the bilateral trade agreement in October 1992 has seen a modest growth in trade to about $250 million in both directions. Agreements have been concluded on taxation, investment, standards, customs, telecommunications, aviation , and in all the areas for facilitating commerce. A binational fund for joint practical scientific and technological research has begun to be available as of 1996, and the construction of an Israeli industrial and technological park in Tianjin is on the drawing boards. The opening of an Israeli Consulate General in Shanghai, in August 1994, was a major step in Israel's efforts to expand her trade and investment activities in China's industrial and commercial east and south-east hubs, particularly in view of the prior existence of an Israeli Consulate General in Hong Kong, which will be in a position to bolster these efforts after mid-1997.

Agricultural co-operation has continued to develop apace, with the establishment of the first joint agricultural demonstration station at Yungledian, in the Beijing area, and of an agricultural training centre on the (Beijing) eastern campus of the China Agricultural University. Additional such centres and stations are in the planning stage. Chinese farmers, instructors, technicians and other professionals attend training courses in Israel in considerable numbers, and mobile courses are conducted in China by Israeli instructors.

On the more visible plane of state visits, no Israeli leader or dignitary has forgone the experience of a visit to China, which had been in its entirety a Forbidden City for Israelis over the decades. However, their successors in office must now await reciprocal visits from their Chinese colleagues. One Chinese Vice Premier and a Foreign Minister have visited Israel, as have a number of other ministers. But Jerusalem still awaits a Chinese Presidential or Prime Ministerial reciprocal visit. Indeed, it is no secret that Israel's current President wishes to visit China and is counselled that he should patiently await a visit of China's President, following the Israeli Presidential visit to China at the end of 1992. Even Israel's Foreign Minister is inhibited by the fact of two visits of Israeli Foreign Ministers to China having been reciprocated by only one such visit from China, as of the end of 1996. However, he is planning another visit to China in early 1997. The sudden 'hiccup' in Israel–China official visits and exchanges, evidenced in the cancellations in the autumn of 1996, has only served to deepen this imbalance.

Despite the significance ascribed to official visits, balance and reciprocity, in the Chinese view of international relations and protocol, both countries stress their close co-operation and understanding. Perhaps the only persistent undercurrents have been Israel's anxiety over Chinese nuclear co-operation with Iran and dissatisfaction with the continuity, or almost imperceptible change in China's support for Arab inspired or initiated anti-Israel resolutions in international forums. On some key, demonstrative issues, such as the 1991 repudiation of the notorious 1975 'Zionism is Racism' resolution and the now-discontinued annual Arab efforts to have the General Assembly reject Israel's credentials, China has moderated her UN voting in Israel's favour. But in general, China tends to constancy, consistency and traditional patterns of voting and positions in international forums, following or leading what remains of the non-aligned bloc. It urges Israel to have patience in these matters, as in those of the peace process, the progress of which will inevitably resolve such other concerns and irritations.

On the question of nuclear and other forms of military co-operation with Iran, China responds to Israel's anxieties at the threat to the peace of the region posed by the fundamentalist regime in Iran, with assurances of its own firm commitment to nuclear non-proliferation, its adherence to the Treaty (NPT) and of the exclusively peaceful purposes to which its co-operation is subject, under the supervision of the International Atomic Energy Agency. Israel has not felt reassured, on this as on denials of reports of China's missile supplies to Iran.

One issue on which China displays maximum international sensitivity, Taiwan, afforded Israel an opportunity, early in 1995, to demonstrate her commitment to the One China policy. The Taiwanese authorities gave publicity to plans for their President, Lee Tenghui, to make a pilgrimage to the holy places in Israel, in the course of a Middle East tour. Although he did visit other capitals in the region, the government of Israel did not permit a visit to Israel. This was greatly appreciated in Beijing and publicly applauded by the Chinese Foreign Ministry spokesman. It did not, however, induce a reciprocity of consideration for Israel's sensitivities when, the following year, the Mayor of Xian invited his Jerusalem counter-part to a conference of Mayors of Ancient Cities, together with the Palestine Authority's man in Jerusalem, Feisal Husseini, thereby conferring a form of recognition of the Palestine Authority's status in the city, oblivious to the fact that Jerusalem has only one mayor. The Jerusalem Mayor rejected the invitation in these circumstances, and strong displeasure was expressed in official and unofficial Jerusalem at what was considered to be damaging, external inter-vention in one of the delicate political issues at the heart of the Israel–Palestinian negotiations and peace process.

The last incident has been an exception, over the course of the first five years of official relations between the two countries. Until the sudden and apparently inconsistent change in China's tactics on the peace process in the autumn of 1996, China's policy seemed set to continue to be one of support for stability and local problem-solving throughout the region, with minimal external and great power interference, as China demonstrated in the international debates which ensued from the flare-up of the Kurdistan problem, in the late summer of 1996. A major Chinese interest lies in obtaining various forms of advanced technology from Israel, as from else-where. In the period under review, there have been two Israeli Chiefs of General Staff of the armed services; both of these have visited China. Another major, strategic Chinese interest must surely be access to international oil supplies. In the early years of the decade, when relations with Israel were established, China was still an oil exporter. This was no longer the case by mid-decade. A Washington DC think-tank estimates that by the year 2010, China will need to import the equivalent of half of Saudi Arabia's total present oil production.[1] Israel, for its part, is likely to continue to foster and develop its relations with the country slated to become the world's greatest economy in the early part of the coming century. Indicative, perhaps, of the significance of China for Israel was the fact that when a Council for the Promotion of Israel–China Relations was inaugu-rated in Tel Aviv in September 1996, Israel's two ex-Presidents and a former Prime Minister were among its sponsors and honorary officers. It may be of some interest in Israel to note what will be the extent and quality of China's reciprocity on this score, too. However, the major disturbing development has been what is optimistically termed in these pages the recent 'hiccup', or temporary aberration from the norm, in China's tactical policy towards Israel and the Middle East peace process.

---

1. 'Between the Dragon and the Deep Blue Sea', *The Economist*, Tomorrow's Japan Survey, 15 July 1996, p.5

Index